HERE WE
STAND

HERE WE STAND

600 Inspiring Messages from the
World's Best Commencement Addresses

Randy Howe

THE LYONS PRESS
GUILFORD, CONNECTICUT

AN IMPRINT OF THE GLOBE PEQUOT PRESS

The Lyons Press is an imprint of The Globe Pequot Press

Text design by Sheryl P. Kober

Library of Congress Cataloging-in-Publication Data is available on file.

ISBN 978-1-59921-567-9

Printed in the United States of America

10 9 8 7 6 5 4 3 2 1

To Noelle and David, I look forward to all of your graduations,
from pre-school to grad school.

CONTENTS

ACKNOWLEDGMENTS

I would like to thank Holly Rubino for keeping me focused and proper. She is a wonderful editor and one reason is, as a former teacher, she always knows how to calmly and confidently point me in the right direction.

I would like to thank my wife, Alicia, for taking such good care of our future grads while I played the role of coffee-chugging, seat-hording writer at Starbucks.

And finally, I would like to thank my parents and my grandmother for being such a big part of all my graduations. Their presence reinforced the notion that an education is worth celebrating!

COMMENCEMENT

Greetings, graduates. This is one of the proudest moments of your life and I am honored to be a part of it, speaking to you as I am through the pages of this book. In truth, it is not me speaking to you, but an amazing collection of accomplished people. Whatever walk of life they came from, one thing binds them together and that is the ability to articulate a thought, both on paper and in speech. Originally, I intended to just skim the 200-plus commencement addresses I'd gathered, but more often than not I found myself reading them from start to finish. I was impressed by the way these speeches so aptly captured the feeling of excitement that permeates every commencement ceremony: one part nostalgia and one part anticipation.

For many of you, this book was a gift from a loved one. It was their way of saying: "I love you," "Good job," "Best of luck," and "That commencement address we just heard wasn't long enough, so here's a book full of more of the same!" The "same" includes wisdom and warnings, reflections and challenges, advice and personal anecdotes, each contributor reflecting back upon their own experiences while pointing you towards the future. In a way, graduation speech quotes are like fortune cookies, bite-sized bits to be enjoyed after the main show has come to a close. I love my Lo Mein, but I really love getting the fortune cookie afterwards. The cookie is never that great—I think it has more to do with getting a fortune that speaks directly to you. Those really are the best quotes, aren't they? The ones that make you feel like someone has lived a life similar to yours and understands not only where you've been but where you're heading? I let that idea guide me as I read through all those speeches.

Nobody knows for sure when the first graduation speech was delivered, but the tradition seems to have started with the students themselves. In the United States, no school is more steeped in tradition than Harvard and its first commencement ceremony was on September 23, 1642. Back then, before a student could graduate, he had to deliver a "Commencement Oration" in Greek, Latin, and/or Hebrew to professors and peers. This was often seen as not just a display of knowledge and rhetorical skills, but as an opportunity for prospective employers to determine a candidate's worth. And as if that wasn't stressful enough, dinner was also served . . . at the expense of those who were graduating! In those early days, there was much drinking to be done—in "Bits of Harvard History," Samuel F. Batchelder claims that eighteen barrels of wine, fourteen barrels of beer, and one barrel of cider were consumed at the ceremony in 1703—and with it came many toasts. The first toast was always the privilege of the governor of Massachusetts and thus the origin of the commencement address as we now know it, delivered by a guest speaker.

It has become the norm for these dignitaries to be granted honorary degrees, and it was at Harvard that the first such honor was bestowed. The year was 1753 and the degree went to Benjamin Franklin. Eighty-five years later, another historical figure took the stage in Harvard Yard. When Ralph Waldo Emerson was invited to speak to the graduates of the Harvard Divinity School, clearly one of his goals was to ensure that his commencement address be more meaningful than ceremonial. He told the crowd that there was a lack of faith in society and referred to "the vulgar tone of preaching." He was critical of "historical Christianity" and its focus on Jesus as a person. In response to this controversial speech, Harvard refused to invite Emerson back to campus and despite being an alumnus he did not return for thirty years. But a norm had been established and ever since, philosophers and politicians have used this platform as an opportunity to share their ideas on important matters. In 1947, Army Chief of Staff George C. Marshall was invited to speak at—you guessed it!—Harvard and decided that this was an appropriate forum for launching his plan to rebuild Western Europe. He described how important it was for the victor to help the vanquished, and within six years time the Marshall Plan was in effect and successful enough to earn Marshall a Nobel Peace Prize. Another Nobel winner, Dr. Martin Luther King, Jr., spoke to the graduating class at Lincoln University on June 6, 1961. Towards the end of his address, King provided a hint of his "I Have a Dream" speech, a speech he would not deliver for another two years. Surely, those fortunate enough to be in the audience knew they were hearing something special. The commencement address has come a long way from the days of barrels of booze in Harvard Yard.

Graduation speeches have been used to decry communism and apartheid, to promote AIDS activism and Habitat for Humanity, to discuss the need for ethics in business and in government. They have often been used to warn graduates away from the kind of materialism that a diploma gives access to and to invite them to start acting like adults. Fortunately, these speeches aren't all doom and gloom. When I graduated high school in 1989, we had co-valedictorians whose GPAs were identical to the ten-thousandth place. Speaking of identical, the co-valedictorians happened to be identical twins, making the occasion all the more newsworthy. The speech was great as Ken and John used all of the different methods suggested to them by family and friends. One paragraph was delivered with alternating words, another with them taking turns at the end of each sentence. I believe they even sang a paragraph! After a few minutes of this, John stepped aside so that Ken could speak about his high school experience and his hopes for the future. Then Ken returned to his seat so that John could speak. Similarly, in 1995 Vermont's most famous purveyors of ice cream delivered a speech in tandem at Southampton College. Ben & Jerry followed Ken & John's model of taking turns rather than going back and forth from one word to the next. Jerry Greenfield spoke first, opting to be brief and congratulatory, humble and funny. Ben Cohen followed, taking more time to eschew the goofiness most often associated with the two ice cream makers. There have been plenty of funny speeches and as you read this book you will laugh along with Will Ferrell and Stephen Colbert—Bill Gates, Sandra Day O'Connor, and Barbara Bush, too, if you can believe it—but for Ben it was important to talk about companies that value people and the world in which they live. This was so important to him, in fact, that he went on to deliver several other addresses on his own.

For Ben, public speaking is easy, but a surprising number of famous, well-educated people have described just how hard it was for them to write their speech. Many were haunted by the memory of an awful address they'd once endured and had to admit to worrying that it might now be their turn to be endured rather than enjoyed. Delivering a speech is stressful, let alone writing one, but I ended up finding more great speeches than I knew what to do with. And what was it they all had in common? They combined relevance and originality.

One example of originality was George Plimpton's speech at—that's right!—Harvard. Plimpton was a writer who cared so much about his readers that he once finagled his way into a golf tournament in order to tell what it was like to play professional golf. One spring training, he took the mound to pitch against major league hitters and one fall he put on a helmet and shoulder pads to play with the Detroit Lions. And lived to tell about it! So it was, in 1997, that he gave Harvard grads the unorthodox order to go back to their rooms. Rather than receive their diplomas, he directed them to "Unpack!" Somewhat tongue-in-cheek, Plimpton was sharing the perspective of the old guard, fearful of all the fine young minds coming out to take all the good jobs and shake up the world. But he was also addressing the palpable air of nostalgia that hangs over every commencement ceremony. Of course Harvard's seniors were excited to get their diplomas, but there was a part of each and every one of them that wanted to retreat; to go back to their rooms and unpack so that they could spend more time with friends and put off the real world for just one more day. Plimpton's degree of empathy is worth noting as this is another important aspect of all good speeches.

Just as those in Harvard Yard must have been thankful for Plimpton's speech, so too were the graduates of Iona College when Mario Cuomo turned the tables and gave advice not to them but to their parents! Cuomo, who was the governor of New York at the time, let the parents know that there wasn't much that they could tell their sons and daughters. The grownups had had their chance and the young people in their caps and gowns were well-prepared to outdo them. Cuomo wasn't all serious business, though. He went so far as to compare commencement speakers to the body at an Irish wake, but you'll have to read on to get that story. I believe you'll find the quote to be both original and relevant.

Speeches are a form of rhetoric and rhetoric, according to Plato, is the "art of enchanting the soul." Without a doubt, the best graduation speeches captivate the audience, heart and soul. They enchant us without smothering. They advise us without being didactic. They remind us that people of all generations are the same while also making Mario Cuomo's point that youth has a leg up on the modern world. The soon-to-be-alumnae are told that there is a road less traveled, but that this road has its tolls. And then they are told that the journey is still worth the expense, so hit the road. They are told to relish the ups and downs because it is better to be six feet above the ground than six feet below it. They are told things they already suspect but with the passing of time will truly come to know. They are told all of these things in a way that they can understand and appreciate. Then, the time of enchanting words comes to an end, the dignitary sits down, the diplomas are distributed, the photos are taken and it is time for lunch. You and your family sit down at the table, at which point somebody passes a present to you and inside is this book, a book that dedicates as many pages to looking forward as it does to looking back. That is because the best commencement addresses capture the essence of graduation, allowing the audience to tune one ear to the celebration of accomplishments while the other hears the call, loud and clear, of what lies ahead.

Randy Howe
Madison, CT
June 2008

Congratulations, Now Go Get 'em!

You are the **universe**
announcing itself to itself.

*—Alan Alda, actor, at the
California Institute of Technology (2002)*

By exploring the mysteries and uncertainties of such a broad range of thought and experience, you have become liberated from the shackles of intellectual narrowness and limitation.

—**Mary Sue Coleman,** university president, at the University of Iowa (2002)

Your education has prepared you for
whatever happens.
—**Roderick Paige,** *secretary of education, at Grambling State University (2001)*

We are terribly proud of you, and we always were, although we've tried to be tasteful about it.

—**Garrison Keillor,** broadcaster and writer, speaking as a figurative parent at Gettysburg College (1987)

So congratulations, good luck, and remember always to sit up straight.

—**Madeleine K. Albright,** secretary of state,
at Wellesley College (1995)

The tassel is worth the hassle.

—*Widely quoted, but author unknown*

This class comes with, I'm sure, a range of emotions that we can only guess at, exhilaration and exhaustion among them. But also, as we've already heard, a lot of gratitude for the opportunities they have been given. And they also deserve from us gratitude for undertaking the rigorous education which they have, for pushing themselves to the limits and now for going into the world ready to use their talents . . .

—**Hillary Rodham Clinton,** politician,
at Harvard Medical School (1998)

I say: You can't dance if you've got too much
muck in your head.
 Let it go.
  Be free,
   and dance through life.
—**Yoko Ono,** artist, at the Maine College of Art (2003)

By giving us a model of individuality, tolerance,
adventure, and risk-taking you have already taught
us a good deal about living fulfilled in the future.
You're the bungee-jumping generation.

—*Anna Quindlen, writer,
at Colgate University (2003)*

Yours has been an education that cannot simply be measured in the tests you've taken or the diploma

you're about to receive. For it has also been an **education in humanity,** brought about by a force of nature—a lesson in both our capacity for good and in the imperfections of man; in our ability to rise to great challenges and our tendency to sometimes fall short of our obligations to one another.

—**Barack Obama,** U.S. president,
at Xavier University (2006)
one year after Hurricane Katrina

In your transition from student to scholar to graduate, our nation is once again blessed with renewed creativity and the power of youthful idealism. For just as surely as each one of you represents the pinnacle of hope and achievement for your families, so, too, do you represent yet one more jewel in the crown of our great democracy.

—**Daniel K. Inouye,** politician,
at the University of Hawaii (1992)

The person who knows **"how"** will always have a job. The person who knows **"why"** will always be his boss.

—**Diane Ravitch,** education professor and author,
at Reed College (1985)

Take a moment every day to make someone in your life a hero. All it takes is a cup of coffee, a smile, a hello on the street, and that ten minutes can turn into a lifetime for someone else.

—**Charlie Rose,** *journalist and talk show host,*
at Colgate University (2002)

Save yourself several thousand dollars and **start flossing** like a maniac now.

—**Callie Khouri,** writer, at Sweet Briar College (1994)

Put the alarm clock in the bathroom.

—*John Walsh, art curator, at Wheaton College (2000)*

Approach your lives as if they were novels, with their own heroes, villains, red herrings, and triumphs.

—**Mary Higgins Clark,** author, at Saint Joseph College (2002)

Computers are insincere.
Books are sincere. And don't try to make yourself an extended family out of ghosts on the Internet. Get yourself a Harley, and join Hell's Angels instead.

—**Kurt Vonnegut,** author, at Agnes Scott College (1999)

As you partake of the world's bill of fare . . .
Do a lot of spitting out the hot air. And be
careful what you swallow.

—**Dr. Seuss,** *children's book author and illustrator,*
at Lake Forest College (1977)

The other advice I have to give you is, do not
live your life safely. I would take risks and not do
things just because everybody else does them.

—**Wilma P. Mankiller,** deputy chief of the Cherokee Nation,
at Northern Arizona University (1992)

Give up the quest for perfection and shoot for five
good minutes in a row.

—**Cathy Guisewite,** cartoonist,
at the University of Michigan (1994)

When you get out there in the world, try not to make it worse than it already is.

—**Russell Baker,** *writer,*
at Connecticut College (1995)

If you are going to have other people work for you . . . you've got to develop the skills, their skills, you've got to motivate them, and you've got to tap their full potential. You manage inventories; you don't manage people. You lead and inspire people.

—**Ross Perot,** businessman and third-party candidate for president,
at Boston University (1994)

If living a **happy life** gives a person the right to advise others on how to live their lives, then I am eminently qualified.

—**Andy Rooney,** broadcaster and writer,
at Colgate University (1996)

*Have a style, by all means **have a style,** but remember that fashion itself has a cold center. There is nothing behind it.*

—**Ken Burns,** *documentary filmmaker,*
at Hampshire College (1987)

The easiest way to be a **big success** is to be able to anticipate what is going to happen in your field and to be there **before it happens** rather than after it happens because that's where the greatest fortunes and successes are made—**doing something before somebody else does it.**

—**Ted Turner,** business and media executive, at the University of North Carolina at Chapel Hill (1993)

... sleep in the nude. In an age when people don't even get dressed up to go to the theater, it's silly getting dressed up to go to bed. What's more, now that you can no longer smoke, drink, or eat bacon and eggs ... sleeping in the nude is one deliciously sinful pleasure you can commit without being caught by the Puritan squads that patrol the nation.

—**Russell Baker,** writer, at Connecticut College (1995)

For every 30 min of TV you watch, **READ** one poem out loud. For every work of literature you read, spend at least 30 min in the mall, or in a mall equivalent such as Wal-Mart. This is cross-fertilization—a new-age form of crop rotation—a way to cross train yr spirit.

—**Suzan-Lori Parks,** writer, at Mount Holyoke College (2001)

Do not bow your heads.

Do not know your place.

Defy the gods.

You will be astonished how many of them turn out to have feet of clay. Be guided, if possible, by your better natures.

—***Salman Rushdie,*** *author,*
at Bard College (1996)

You make a list this afternoon, of the people who don't believe in you, and you call them tonight, and **tell them to go to hell!**

—**Ray Bradbury,** author,
at the California Institute of Technology (2000)

One last piece of advice, never say you'll give a talk unless you know clearly what you're going to talk about and more or less what you're going to say.

—**Richard Feynman,** physicist,
at the California Institute of Technology (1974)

Self-confidence, a quiet self-confidence not cockiness not conceit not arrogance, is the key to winning, to excelling, no matter what you do in life.

—**David L. Calhoun,** corporate executive,
at Virginia Tech University (2005)

I submit that you throw out all previous notions of one career followed by a lazy retirement. That was the strategy of your grandfathers and it's strictly wheelchair thinking. You need a new strategy for a lifetime of alertness that lasts a whole century.

—**David Mahoney,** *corporate executive,*
at Rutgers University (1996)

Remember, we're from Jersey. We've been the underdogs all our lives. And I can tell you this: It's passion, not pedigree, that can and will win in the end. Free yourself from comparison. Just because someone has fancy sneakers doesn't mean they can run faster.

—**Jon Bon Jovi,** musician, at Monmouth University (2001)

If ever there was a time to take a chance on yourself—to take some risks, to see what you are capable of and what your destiny may be—
the time is now.

—**Charles Schumer,** politician,
at the State University College at Oswego (2002)

Be as bold as the first man or woman to eat an oyster.

—*Shirley Chisholm, politician,*
at Mount Holyoke College (1981)

You are our best hope for the future.
Don't blow it.

—**Lloyd Bentsen,** politician,
at Texas A&M University (1985)

When I was a kid in Dublin, I watched in awe as America put a man on the moon and thought, wow—this is mad! Nothing is impossible in America! . . . Is that still true? Tell me it's true. It is true, isn't it? And if it isn't, you of all people can make it true again.

—**Bono,** musician,
at Harvard University (2001)

Welcome to the fire—
now it is your turn to hold the hose.

—**Billy Joel,** *musician,*
at Fairfield University (1991)

Playing ball or practicing law, a person gets just an occasional opportunity to do something great. To come through in a big way. When the time comes, just two things matter. How well prepared we are to seize the moment. And having the courage to take our best swing.

—**Hank Aaron,** baseball Hall of Famer and civil rights advocate,
at Emory University School of Law (1995)

God bless you—God bless you as much as God blessed us when he sent you along. Thank you so much, and now go and do good.

—**Garrison Keillor,** broadcaster and writer,
at Gettysburg College (1987)

This is your time. *Take it on. Don't be afraid to lean into the wind, love the earth in all of its natural glories and take care of each other.* *We're counting on you.*

—*Tom Brokaw, broadcaster,*
at Connecticut College (1996)

I would urge you to be as imprudent as you dare.

Be Bold!
Be Bold!
Be Bold!

—**Susan Sontag,** author, screenwriter, and director,
at Wellesley College (1983)

To live life at its fullest you have to have the chutzpah to accept challenges. You don't need nerves of steel. I'm not saying that sometimes you won't be shaking in your boots after accepting some major challenge. But you can't let that stop you.

—**Ruth Westheimer,** sex therapist and talk show host,
at Trinity College (2004)

It's great to plan for your future. Just don't live there, because really nothing ever happens in the future. Whatever happens happens now, so live your life where the action is—now.

—**Jerry Zucker,** director and producer,
at the University of Wisconsin (2003)

If you want to play a game, go to where it's played and find a way to get in. Things happen when you **get in the game.**

—**Chris Matthews,** talk show host,
at Montgomery College (2006)

So go on and do the thing that scares the hell out of you, because in this world, not unlike Hollywood, the gamble is almost as safe a bet as the sure thing.

—*Callie Khouri, writer,*
at Sweet Briar College (1994)

In a study done by an economist at Berkeley, it was found that anytime it's 4th down and 4, or closer than 4 yards, you should go for it.

DO NOT PUNT!

Don Shula himself, the winningest coach in NFL history, a man who grew up here in northern Ohio, was once asked, "Is there any big innovation left in football?" Shula said, "Someday there will be a coach that doesn't punt."

—**Brian Kenny,** sportscaster,
at Ohio Northern University (2007)

In football we always said that the other team couldn't beat us. We had to be sure that we didn't beat ourselves. And that's what people have to do, too—make sure they don't beat themselves.

—**Woody Hayes,** football coach,
at the Ohio State University (1986)

*My favorite animal is the turtle. The reason is that in order for the turtle to move, it has to **stick its neck out.** There are going to be times in your life when you're going to have to stick your neck out. There will be **challenges** and instead of hiding in a shell, you have to **go out and meet them!***

—*Ruth Westheimer, sex therapist and talk show host,*
at Trinity College (2004)

At the end of your days, you will be judged by your gallop, not by your stumble.

—**Bradley Whitford,** actor,
at the University of Wisconsin (2006)

The fireworks begin today. Each diploma is a lighted match. Each one of you is a fuse.

—**Edward Koch,** politician,
at the Polytechnic Institute of New York (1983)

The world of the 90s . . . will belong to passionate, driven leaders—people who not only have an enormous amount of energy but who can energize those whom they lead.

—**Jack Welch,** CEO of General Electric, in several commencement speeches

Just keep trying! Never give up, never, never give up! Because the only person that can stop you is . . . you!

—*Yvonne Thorton, author,
at Tuskegee University (2003)*

Whatever you do, help us love science the way you do. Like the young man so head over heels about his sweetheart he can't stop talking about her, like the young woman so in love with her young man she wants everyone to know how wonderful he is ... show us pictures, tell us stories, make us crave to meet your beloved.

—**Alan Alda,** actor,
at the California Institute of Technology (2002)

But the **challenges that we face** cannot be met by government alone. We can only fulfill the promise of this revolution if we **work together** in the same way it was launched together, with creativity, resolve, and a restless spirit of innovation.

—**Bill Clinton,** U.S. president,
discussing the Technology Revolution
at the Massachusetts Institute of Technology (1998)

But I do want you to be an actor in your own life. Infuse your life with action.

Don't wait for it to happen. Make it happen. Make your own future. Make your own hope. Make your own love.

And whatever your beliefs, honor your creator, not by passively waiting for grace to come down from upon high, but by doing what you can to make grace happen . . .

—**Bradley Whitford,** actor,
at the University of Wisconsin (2006)

Find Yourself, Challenge Yourself

We say about **people** with a *passion*
that they "lose themselves" in their work.
Which really means, in another sense, that they
find themselves in their **work**.

—*Marvin Bell,* poet,
at Alfred University (2002)

Look in the mirror tonight. Who is that man? Who is that woman? She is the work of your life. He is its greatest glory . . .

—**Anna Quindlen,** writer,
at Colgate University (2003)

As you work to **find your passion,** you should know that sometimes, your passion just finds you.

—**Condoleezza Rice,** secretary of state,
at Boston College (2006)

Young ladies and gentlemen, this is not your world yet. You have to make it.

—**Bill Cosby,** actor and comedian,
at the University of South Carolina (1986)

Try brushing your teeth tonight with your other hand.

—**Ken Burns,** *documentary filmmaker,*
at Skidmore College (2002)

There is a need for physicians, scientists, and others who have concern for human life to work together towards improving health and well-being in all of its dimensions. If we do not, who will be to blame for the future, to which we and our ancestors will have contributed? How will we be looked back upon by those who follow?

—**Jonas Salk,** research scientist,
at Harvard University Medical School (1991)

When I look back and think about the things I could have done and should have done and wish I had said and wanted to try and thought of changing, time and time again I see the only brick walls that were ever really in my way were the ones I lovingly built myself, brick by brick, and then proceeded to smash my head against.

—**Cathy Guisewite,** cartoonist,
at the University of Michigan (1994)

This country desperately needs more wise and courageous shepherds and fewer sheep who do not borrow from integrity to fund expediency.

—**Marian Wright Edelman,** *founder of the Children's Defense Fund, at Washington University (1992)*

And **don't ever be afraid** of high expectations. A great heritage is like something we can't escape, even if we want to. It's like a foundation under our feet, we didn't put it there, but we're standing on it anyway. And either we build on the foundation, or it will crumble away underneath us.

—**Hank Aaron,** baseball Hall of Famer and civil rights advocate, at Emory University School of Law (1995)

With curiosity comes fearlessness. A child will walk up to a hot stove and touch it. Does it hurt? Yes! Was it a stupid thing to do? Well, kind of. But you have to admire the daring of that child. His brave spirit is the angel inside each of us, the force that often seems to shrink as we grow bigger.

—**Steven Spielberg,** director and producer, at the University of Southern California (1994)

Since death is real and inevitable for all of us, how then should we live our lives? For me the answer to this question has been clear since I was young: We should commit ourselves to following our hearts and doing what we most love and what we most want to do in life.

—**John Mackey,** corporate executive, at Bentley College (2008)

You need to be absolutely paranoid about the currency of your knowledge and ask yourself every day: am I really up to speed? Or am I stagnating intellectually, faking it or even worse, falling behind? Am I still learning? Or am I just doing the same stuff on a different day . . .

—**David L. Calhoun,** corporate executive,
at Virginia Tech University (2005)

Probably the most dangerous thing about an **academic education**—*at least in my own case—is that it enables my tendency to over-intellectualize stuff, to get lost in abstract argument inside my head, instead of simply* **paying attention** *to what is going on right in front of me, paying attention* **to what is going on inside me.**

—**David Foster Wallace,** writer,
at Kenyon College (2005)

Self-sufficiency
is an extremely worthwhile goal.

—**Callie Khouri,** writer,
at Sweet Briar College (1994)

The thing that is really hard, and really amazing, is giving up on being perfect and beginning the work of becoming yourself.

—**Anna Quindlen,** writer, at Mount Holyoke (1999)

You have to leave the city of your comfort and go into the wilderness of your intuition. You can't get there by bus, only by hard work and risk and by not quite knowing what you're doing, but what you'll discover will be wonderful. What you'll discover will be yourself.

—**Alan Alda,** actor, at Connecticut College (1980)

There's no there. That elusive "there" with the job, the beach house, the dream, it's not out there. There is here. It's in you . . . right now.

—**Brian Kenny,** *sportscaster, at Ohio Northern University (2007)*

At commencement you wear your square-shaped mortarboards. My hope is that from time to time you will let your minds be bold, and wear sombreros.

—**Paul Freund,** Harvard Law school professor

Don't live down to expectations.
Go out there and
do something remarkable.

—**Wendy Wasserstein,** playwright

But this I do know: You have a first-class education from a first-class school. And so you need not, probably cannot, live a "paint-by-numbers" life.

—***Barbara Bush,*** *First Lady,*
at Wellesley College (1990)

While there is nothing that builds confidence more than winning against the odds, believe it or not, losing against great odds builds it as well. Most great companies love people who take big swings even if they have to walk back to the dugout on occasion and sit down.

—**David L. Calhoun,** corporate executive,
at Virginia Tech University (2005)

We are all children
in various stages of growing up.

—**Doug Marlette,** editorial cartoonist,
at Wesleyan University (2005)

The moment between completing one chapter in life and beginning the next generally produces a mixture of reflection, relief, and regret.

—**Mary Robinson,** president of Ireland,
at Emory University (2004)

You have reached a stepping-stone in your life, a place where you can pause for a moment and enjoy the luxury of looking back on the distance covered; but the thing about stepping-stones is that you always need to find another one up there ahead of you. Even if it is panicky in mid-stream, there is no going back. The next move is always the test.

—**Seamus Heaney,** poet,
at the University of North Carolina at Chapel Hill (1996)

A commencement is a time of joy. It is also a time of melancholy. But then again, so is life.

—**Paul Tsongas,** politician,
at Massachusetts Institute of Technology (1989)

The greatest story you will ever tell is your own.

—**Charlie Rose,** journalist and talk show host,
at Colgate University (2002)

*Insist on having a past,
and then you will have a future.*

—**Ken Burns,** *documentary filmmaker,
at Case Western Reserve University (1993)*

We don't beat the reaper by living longer.
We beat the reaper by living well and living fully.

—**Randy Pausch,** professor of computer science and author
of *The Last Lecture,* at Carnegie Mellon (2008)

Fall in love with the process
and the results will follow.

—**Bradley Whitford,** actor,
at the University of Wisconsin (2006)

Remembering that you are going to die
is the best way I know to avoid the trap of
thinking you have something to lose.
You are already naked.
There is no reason not to follow your heart.

—**Steve Jobs,** CEO of Apple Computers,
at Stanford University (2005)

So, as we say at the NFL Draft, *"You're on the clock."* Your life is well underway. At the same time, I think it's important to heed to the advice of Basketball Coach John Wooden. Wooden, who coached UCLA to 10 NCAA Championships and has one himself as a player told his teams:

"LIVE as though you'll die tomorrow.
LEARN as though you'll live forever."

—*Brian Kenny, sportscaster,*
at Ohio Northern University (2007)

And he [Harvard psychologist Erik Erikson] taught us that the **richest and fullest lives attain an inner balance of work, love and play,** in equal order, that to pursue one to the disregard of others is to open oneself to ultimate sadness in older age, whereas to pursue all three with equal dedication is to make possible an old age filled with **serenity, peace and fulfillment.**

—**Doris Kearns Goodwin,** presidential historian,
at Dartmouth College (1998)

I still get up at five-thirty every morning because I **like my life so much** *that I hate to waste any of it by sleeping more than is necessary.*

—**Andy Rooney,** broadcaster and writer,
at Colgate University (1996)

It is so easy to waste our lives: our days, our hours, our minutes. It is so easy to take for granted the color of the azaleas, the sheen of the limestone on Fifth Avenue, the color of our kid's eyes, the way the melody in a symphony rises and falls and disappears and rises again. It is so easy to exist instead of live.

—**Anna Quindlen,** writer,
at Villanova University (2000)

We also frequently make the mistake of believing that if we forgive others we are also condoning their harmful behavior. However, forgiveness simply means to relinquish our resentment and anger toward others, it doesn't mean relinquishing our values and ethics. When we forgive others we free ourselves from the past and allow our hearts to be fully in the present moment, which is where love exists.

—**John Mackey,** corporate executive, at Bentley College (2008)

Commencement Fact

Back in the 16th century, Oxford University was the first school to make the mortar board a part of its commencement ceremony. It is believed that this cap is square either because that was the shape of the Oxford campus or, more likely, because it is reminiscent of a book and therefore looks scholarly. Originally called a "biretta," which is a stiff hat worn by Roman Catholic clerics, the name "mortar board" soon came into fashion because it so closely resembles the tool used by bricklayers to hold their mortar.

The Journey, Both Literal and Figurative

For over the years

I have learned that life is a voyage of *discovery* and not a safe harbor. It is on the voyage that we learn how to steer our own lives and with them the life of the nation we love.

—*Katherine D. Ortega,* treasurer of the United States, at Kean State College (1985)

Your childhood is spent dreaming, your young adulthood preparing.

—**Robert D. Ballard,** oceanographer and founder of the JASON project, at the Worcester Polytechnic Institute (1992)

We do not know the beginning
or the end,
we only see the middle of things
which is our own life.

—**Alice Walker,** *writer,*
at Agnes Scott College (1997)

Embrace the **unknown.**

—**Guy Kawasaki,** businessman,
at Palo Alto High School (1995)

If you're sitting out there now with
*a **nice, neat little outline** for the*
next ten years, you'd better be careful.
Life may have other plans.

—*John Grisham, author,*
at Mississippi State University (1992)

The reality is that each one of you
will need to rely on your
own moral compass to find your paths.

—**Mary Robinson,** *president of Ireland,*
at Emory University (2004)

... relish the fact that the road of yr life will probably
be a windy road. Something like—the yellow brick
road in the WIZARD OF OZ.
You see the glory of OZ up ahead—but there
are lots of twists and turns along the way—
lots of tin men, lots of green women.

—**Suzan-Lori Parks,** writer,
at Mount Holyoke College (2001)

It is clear that each of us has particular
affinities sensed intuitively through our feelings
of satisfaction as well as through the effects
produced by our actions and the successes
achieved. We need to follow our inclinations
in this regard.

—**Jonas Salk,** research scientist,
at Harvard University Medical School (1991)

You might never fail on the scale I did, but some failure in life is inevitable. It is impossible to live without failing at something, unless you live so cautiously that you might as well not have lived at all—in which case, you fail by default.

—**JK Rowling,** *author,*
at Harvard University (2008)

One of the interesting aspects of age is perspective, getting to see how human behavior cuts across all walks of human life . . . and allows us, if and when we choose, to see ourselves as having more in common with our fellow man than we would like to believe.

—**Paul Michael Glaser,** actor, director, and AIDS activist,
at the Stanford University School of Medicine (2004)

As this great university has recognized, in the foreign students it has attracted, the research it conducts, the courses it offers, and the sensibility it conveys, those of you who have graduated today will live global lives. **You will compete in a world marketplace;** travel further and more often than any previous generation; share ideas, tastes and experiences with counterparts from every culture; and recognize that to have a full and rewarding future, you will have to look outwards.

—**Madeleine K. Albright,** secretary of state, at Harvard University (1997)

The road less traveled is sometimes fraught with barricades, bumps, and uncharted terrain. But it is on that road where your character is truly tested.

—**Katie Couric,** broadcaster, at Williams College (2007)

Move to, or experience, a foreign country as early as you can in your career if you have not already. Go to China, to Southeast Asia, to North Africa, or to India. That is where the future is.

—**David L. Calhoun,** CEO of GE Transportation, at Virginia Tech (2005)

Graduation is only a concept. In real life every day you graduate. Graduation is a process that goes on until the last day of your life. If you can grasp that, you'll make a difference.

—**Arie Pencovici,** social worker

It is indeed ironic that we spend our school days yearning to graduate and our remaining days waxing nostalgic about our school days.

—**Isabel Waxman**

You choose how things affect you. You always have that freedom, no matter how much your liberty it curtailed. You . . . get to choose . . . how things affect you.

—**Patton Oswalt,** comedian, at his alma mater, Broad Run High School (2008)

Party hearty.

Sleep late.

Work hard.

Love someone better than yourself.
Give all to the present
and the future will take care of itself.

*—**Anna Quindlen,** writer,*
at Colgate University (2003)

It is critical that you continually assess where you are in all facets of your life, determine where you want to go, and set goals that you wish to achieve. But remember, **achieving your goals** is not your destination, just part of your journey.

—**Florence Griffith Joyner,** Olympic track star,
at American University (1994)

Let yourself regraduate every four years. In one of my mother's really annoying moments of being right about something, **Mom told me that life deserves an overhaul every four years.** She said four years is exactly enough time in any situation to know what is working, what is not, what is worth saving, and what or who you ought to dump.

—**Cathy Guisewite,** cartoonist,
at the University of Michigan (1994)

It is certain, if you aim high enough, that you will find your strongest beliefs ridiculed and challenged; principles that you cherish may be derisively dismissed by those claiming to be more practical or realistic than you. But no matter how weary you may become in persuading others to see the value in what you value, have courage still—and persevere.

—**Madeleine K. Albright,** secretary of state,
at Mount Holyoke College (1997)

Always take a stand for yourself.

—*Oprah Winfrey, talk show host,
at Howard University (2007)*

You need to get out there and travel, and figure out where you thrive. Some places you'll go to and you'll feel yourself wither . . . If you belong by the ocean, then the mountains will ruin you. If you're suited for the blue solitude of the plains, then the city will be a tight, roaring prison cell that'll eat you alive.

—**Patton Oswalt,** comedian,
at his alma mater, Broad Run High School (2008)

Achievable goals:
the first step towards personal improvement.

—**JK Rowling,** author,
at Harvard University (2008)

Ask yourself one question: If I didn't have to do it perfectly, what would I try?

—**Jerry Zucker,** director and producer,
at the University of Wisconsin (2003)

Believe that the sort of life you wish to live is, at this very moment, just waiting for you to summon it up. **And when you wish for it,** you begin moving toward it, and it, in turn, begins moving toward you.

—**Suzan-Lori Parks,** playwright,
at Mount Holyoke (2001)

If you're going to pray for anything in your life, pray that you be put on your proper path, because life lived with a sense of purpose and commitment is just a lot more rewarding than one that drifts.

—**Callie Khouri,** writer,
at Sweet Briar College (1994)

But the standards of success in the **new world** *are less clear. Here, too, an inner compass is required to select the* **right goals,** *establish accountability, and* **fulfill potential.**

—**Madeleine K. Albright,** secretary of state,
at Wellesley College (1995)

You must resolve to grow intellectually, morally, technically, and professionally every day through your entire work and family life.

—**David L. Calhoun,** corporate executive,
at Virginia Tech University (2005)

Stumbling is not a bad thing—it means that you were on the move, instead of sitting down doing nothing.

—**George Pataki,** *politician,*
at Colgate University (1998)

When you hit a closed door
and it doesn't open easily,
don't get discouraged.
Just rear back and
kick the door open.

—**Muriel Siebert,** stock broker,
at Case Western Reserve University (1998)

Our number one problem is that not enough of us really believe that significant change is possible.

—**Wendy Kopp,** founder of Teach for America,
at Syracuse University (1992)

Life rewards those who, having failed, and having failed over and over, still manage to move on. It is the decision to try again that will ultimately lead to a reward.

—**Fay Vincent,** commissioner of Major League Baseball,
at Kenyon College (1999)

Getting started, keeping going, getting
started again—in art and in life, it seems
to me this is the essential rhythm not only
of achievement but of survival, the ground
of convinced action, the basis of self-esteem
and the guarantee of credibility in your lives,
credibility to yourselves as well as to others.

—**Seamus Heaney,** poet,
at the University of North Carolina at Chapel Hill (1996)

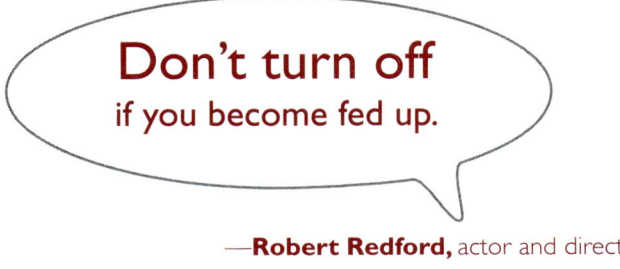

Don't turn off
if you become fed up.

—**Robert Redford,** actor and director,
at Bard College (2004)

And when you fail, and are defeated, and in pain,
and in the dark, then I **hope you will remember**
that **darkness is your country,** where you live,
where **no wars are fought and no wars are won,** but
where the future is.

—**Ursula K. Le Guin,** writer,
at Mills College (1983)

You get it [strength] by going back and getting a new play and running that play together. "Together" is the thing that gives you the build-up to get ready to go again. And in your lifetime, how well you can work with people will depend on how quickly you get back to them and get together.

—**Woody Hayes,** football coach,
at Ohio State University (1986)

I am not dull enough to suppose that because you are young, gifted and well-educated, you have never known hardship or heartbreak. **Talent and intelligence never yet inoculated anyone against the caprice of the Fates,** and I do not for a moment suppose that everyone here has enjoyed an existence of unruffled privilege and contentment.

—**JK Rowling,** author,
at Harvard University (2008)

Whenever you are discouraged — and you will be involved in all kinds of fights for injustice where you live and where you work and on a broader geographical plane — just think of your forebears, think what they did, think of your own absorption of the many problems and injustices that we should be addressing if we were a more serious society.

—**Ralph Nader,** public advocate,
at Bucknell University (2004)

Turn your wounds into wisdom.

—***Oprah Winfrey,*** *talk show host,*
at Wellesley College (1997)

You must have a high threshold for frustration. Take it from the guy who was turned down by every studio in Hollywood. You must knock on doors until your knuckles bleed.

—**Michael Uslan,** producer,
at Indiana University (2006)

There are times when you are going to do well, and times when you're going to fail. But neither the doing well, nor the failure is the measure of success. The measure of success is what you think about what you've done.

—**Marc S. Lewis,** professor of psychology,
at the University of Texas at Austin (2000)

Persistence is critical. Being creative and persistent is even better.

—**Katie Couric,** broadcaster,
at Williams College (2007)

I believe most passionately that in each one of you lies a Jefferson, a Lincoln, an Eleanor Roosevelt, a Mother Teresa, and a Martin Luther King, Jr. None of these great men and women accepted the failures and inequities of the world in which they were born, and neither should you!

—**Daniel K. Inouye,** politician,
at the University of Hawaii (1992)

To the best and the brightest again, just remember to keep it in perspective. Somewhere on the streets of India right now a person brighter than you is starving to death. You're the luckiest person in the world because you happen to be here.

—**Ross Perot,** *businessman and third-party candidate for president, at Boston University (1994)*

Each generation sees farther than the generation that preceded it because it stands on the shoulders of that generation. You're going to have opportunities beyond anything that we've ever known . . .

—**Ronald Reagan,** U.S. president,
at the University of Notre Dame (1981)

It is men and women who have made the world, and they have made it in spite of their gods.

—*Salman Rushdie, author,
at Bard College (1996)*

I've been taking a close look at these graduates. They are actually **taller, stronger, smarter** than we were, smart enough maybe to take our **mistakes as their messages,** to make our **weaknesses their lessons,** and to make our example—**good and not so good**—part of their education.

—**Mario Cuomo,** politician,
at Iona College (1984)

I believe that if you can learn to focus on what you have, you will always see that the universe is abundant and you will have more. If you concentrate and focus in your life on what you don't have, you will never have enough.

—**Oprah Winfrey,** talk show host,
at Wellesley College (1997)

*By all reckoning, the **bumblebee is aerodynamically unsound** and shouldn't be able to fly. Yet, the little bee gets those wings going like a turbo-jet and flies to every plant its chubby little body can land on to collect all the nectar it can hold. Bumblebees are the most persistent creatures. **They don't know they can't fly,** so they just keep buzzing around.*

—***Earl Bakken,*** *corporate executive,*
at the University of Hawaii (2004)

History is full of much cruelty and suffering and darkness and it can be hard sometimes to believe that a brighter future is indeed dawning. But for all of our past failings, for all of our current problems, more people now enjoy lives of hope and opportunity than ever before in all of human history. This progress has been the concerted effort not of cynics but of visionaries and optimists ...

—**Condoleezza Rice,** secretary of state,
at Boston College (2006)

Don't ever rob a bank. Enjoy life. Have fun. Choose to be happy now; don't wait until you're "successful," because honestly, I was as happy when we were unemployed and scrounging around for a buck.

—**Peter Farrelly,** movie director,
at Roger Williams University (2007)

I also want to tell you that no matter what success I had it wouldn't have happened if it wouldn't have been for America, because I tell you, this truly is the land of opportunity. **There is no other place in the world like America.** I have traveled all over the world and I have seen it to be the land of opportunities.

—**Arnold Schwarzenegger,** bodybuilder, actor, and governor,
at Brentwood High School (2008)

People kept dreaming, and building, and working, and marching, and petitioning their government, until they made America a land where the question of our place in history is not answered for us. It's answered by us.

—**Barack Obama,** U.S. president,
at Knox College (2005)

Never give in to pessimism. Don't know that you can't fly, and you will soar like an eagle. Don't end up regretting what you did not do because you were too lazy or too frightened to soar. **Be a bumblebee!** *And soar to the heavens. You can do it.*

—**Earl Bakken,** *corporate executive,*
at the University of Hawaii (2004)

You're only human, so learn to forgive yourself the little things, and do the best you can on the big things. **No one is perfect,** and expecting perfection from yourself or anyone else is a **waste of time.**

—**Callie Khouri,** writer,
at Sweet Briar College (1994)

You have brains in your head/You have feet in your shoes. You can steer yourself in any direction you choose. You're on your own/And you know what you know/You are the guy who'll decide where to go.

—**Dr. Seuss,** *children's book author and illustrator, from* Oh, The Places You'll Go

I can accept failure.
Everybody fails at something.
But I can't accept not trying.

—**Michael Jordan,** basketball player

Self-pity is a remarkably self-destructive emotion, which you should consciously work to eliminate from your emotional life because it dis-empowers you and moves you away from being able to **follow your heart.**

—**John Mackey,** corporate executive, at Bentley College (2008)

Too often, **cynicism can be the fellow traveler of learning** and I understand why.

—**Condoleezza Rice,** secretary of state,
at Boston College (2006)

But if it's true that this is the best time of your life, if you have already lived or are now living at this age the best years, or if the next few turn out to be the best, then you have my condolences. Because you'll want to remain here, stuck in these so-called best years, never maturing, wanting only to look, to feel, and be the adolescent that whole industries are devoted to forcing you to remain.

—**Toni Morrison,** author,
at Wellesley College (2004)

Think of the world as a big glass of water with some salt in it. You have a choice. You can try to pick out all the salt or you can keep pouring in more water so eventually it gets less bitter. As you begin your new journey, you can try to remove everything that you find distasteful in the world, or you can just pour in more love. It's the only thing that the more you give away, the more you have.

—**Jerry Zucker,** director and producer,
at the University of Wisconsin (2003)

Commencement Fact

"Pomp and Circumstance" was composed by Sir Edward Elgar and was one of his five popular Pomp and Circumstance Marches. "Pomp and Circumstance" is the first of these marches and was premiered on October 19, 1901. The "Pomp and Circumstance" name comes from a line in William Shakespeare's Othello.

We learn to *coexist with our fears,* to surmount the obstacles before us. We find ways to defy danger, even as we reach deep **within ourselves** for solutions to the challenges of the age.

—*Katherine D. Ortega,* treasurer of the United States, at Kean State College (1985)

The Importance of Education

I believe that **education** is like an instrument.
Whether that instrument, that device,
is used **properly** or *constructively*
or in a different way depends on the user.

—**The Dalai Lama,** spiritual leader,
at Emory University (1998)

So long as books are kept open,
then minds can never be closed.

—**Katherine D. Ortega,** treasurer of the United States,
at Kean State College (1985)

*We need to slow the tempo of our lives and
extend the **span of our attention.** We need
to emphasize a form of **humane education**
that helps students to establish a **rich
interior life** and an enduring openness of
mind.*

—*James O. Freedman, college president,
at the University of Rochester (2002)*

If you walk out of here with a diploma
in your hand, you better walk out of here with
something these professors put in your heads, too.
And retain it, or you're going to be in bad trouble.

—**Pearl Bailey,** musician,
at Syracuse University (1985)

Education does not develop your character until it merges with integrity and wisdom.

—**Sam Nunn,** politician,
at Emory University (1981)

Education brings light and awareness to the shadows around us.

—*Harold Morse, founder of The Learning Channel,*
at the State University at Oswego (2002)

Remember that your most rewarding moments happened when you learned something new.

—**Edwin Dorn,** university dean,
at the University of Texas at Austin (2002)

It is impossible to break America down into classes in the old European sense. But there is sheerly dividing line and above that line are those who have bachelor's degrees or better from a four-year university or college, and below that line are people who don't.

—**Tom Wolfe,** author,
at Duke University (2002)

The human race is struggling for survival every day, and our only weapon is knowledge. It is the shell on our backs, the poison in our fangs, and the camouflage that covers our bodies.

—**George Lucas,** director,
at the University of Southern California (1994)

You have gained facts and skills, and I hope that there is a strong underpinning of wisdom, and nudging the wisdom aside is a sense of adventure, which I hope you will have.

—**Frank McCourt,** teacher and memoirist,
at Connecticut College (1999)

Draw strength from the knowledge that education will break the backs of poverty, disenfranchisement, and violence: that war is never inevitable but only a terrible failure of the imagination; and that love is stronger than hatred.

—**Wally Lamb,** writer,
at Connecticut College (2003)

When the education of youth goes wrong, sooner or later all goes wrong.

—*Henry Wallace,* U.S. vice president,
at Connecticut College (1943)

A vast system of mental lobotomization has been put into operation that sets the standards to which all accede. (I am speaking, of course, of American television.)

—**Susan Sontag,** writer and director,
at Wellesley College (1983)

Your education is a dress rehearsal for a life that is yours to lead.

—**Nora Ephron,** screenwriter,
at Wellesley College (1996)

A man who has never gone to school may steal from a freight car; but if he has a university education, he may steal the whole railroad.

—**Theodore Roosevelt,** U.S. president

The man who graduates today and stops learning tomorrow is uneducated the day after.

—**Newton D. Baker,** politician

When you leave here, don't forget why you came.

—**Adlai Stevenson,** politician, at Princeton University (1954)

You haven't been taught what to think, but rather, **how** to think, **how** to ask questions, **how** to reject assumptions, **how** to seek knowledge; in short, **how** to exercise reason. This experience will sustain you for the rest of your lives, but no one should assume that a life of reason is easy; to the contrary. It takes a great deal of courage and honesty.

—**Condoleezza Rice,** secretary of state,
at Boston College (2006)

Culture is not enough. There must be an ethical dimension to whatever you study.

—**Elie Wiesel,** author and chair of the president's
Commission on the Holocaust,
at Hobart and William Smith Colleges (1982)

I think it is a mistake to narrowly focus your interests. The broader your experience, the more you can go with the flow, as time goes on.

—*Robert D. Ballard, oceanographer
and founder of the JASON project,
at the Worcester Polytechnic Institute (1992)*

Perhaps the most useful suggestion I can make on the day when most of you are ceasing to be students, is that you go on being students— for the rest of your lives. **Don't move to a mental slum.**

—**Susan Sontag,** author, screenwriter, and director, at Wellesley College (1983)

But the unfortunate, yet truly exciting thing about your life, is that there is no core curriculum. The entire place is an elective. The paths are infinite and the results uncertain.

—**Jon Stewart,** talk show host and comedian, at the College of William and Mary (2004)

From now on, you had better put yourself in charge of your own education, if you haven't already.

—*John Walsh,* art curator, at Wheaton College (2000)

Our graduate schools produce a lot of half-baked bread in the interest of getting it on the shelf quicker. **Don't let the weaknesses of the system become weaknesses of your own.**

—**John Walsh,** art curator,
at Wheaton College (2000)

*For the only way that you will grow intellectually is by **examining your opinions,** attacking your prejudices constantly and completely with the force of your reason.*

—**Condoleezza Rice,** *secretary of state,
at Boston College (2006)*

In the interest of the community, the community instructs the young in the ways of the past; and if I have one superstition, my superstition is that we had better honor those before us as we hope to be honored by those to whom we pass on our treasures of knowledge and skill.

—**Robert Pinsky,** poet,
at Stanford University (1999)

Wellesley is a gift to any woman *who is willing to open her mind and her heart to it . . .*

—**Oprah Winfrey,** talk show host,
at Wellesley College (1997)

I hope that you will place your own energies and any pressures at your disposal to making this college a women's college, and not a school for girls.

—**Gloria Steinem,** feminist, writer, and publisher,
at Smith College (1971)

My first time ever to see Notre Dame was to come here as a sports announcer, two years out of college, to broadcast a football game. You won or I wouldn't have mentioned it.

—**Ronald Reagan,** U.S. president,
at the University of Notre Dame (1981)

Suddenly—they're everywhere—challenging old ideas, giving their lives for peace, discovering medicine, making you laugh hysterically on a cable show, getting indicted for felonies . . . Yale graduates keep affecting your world no matter how loud you turn up the MTV. They're out there wreaking havoc for eternity.

—**Jodie Foster,** actress,
at her alma mater, Yale University (1993)

It might be said now that I have the best of both worlds: a Harvard education and a Yale degree.

—*John F. Kennedy, U.S. president, upon receiving his honorary degree at Yale University (1962)*

And to the degree that a human being can love an institution, I love this place.

—**Randy Pausch,** professor of computer science and author of *The Last Lecture,* at Carnegie Mellon (2008)

Remember the **beauty** *and* **strength** *of this place and let it always be an inspiration to you. Remember the solid,* **gray granite of these walls** *and how these stones have stood against* **countless seasons,** *a symbol of America's strength around the crucible of her military leadership.*

—**Colin Powell,** *chairman of the Joint Chiefs of Staff, at the United States Military Academy (1990)*

This is the place where I learned to love this life, to curse this life, and to claim this life for my very own.

—**Jodie Foster,** actress, at her alma mater, Yale University (1993)

You walk in the tradition of Eisenhower and MacArthur, Patton and Bradley—the commanders who saved a civilization. . . **Graduates of this academy have brought creativity and courage to every field of endeavor.** West Point produced the chief engineer of the Panama Canal, the mind behind the Manhattan Project, the first American to walk in space. This fine institution gave us the man they say invented baseball, and other young men over the years who perfected the game of football.

—**George W. Bush,** U.S. president,
at the United States Military Academy (2002)

This is a school that understands that every hope, every dream, and every single speck of your fabulous education still has to be filtered through you.

. . . That your ability to cope daily with the little stuff is going to have as much to do with how your future works as the four years you just spent getting your degree.

—**Cathy Guisewite,** cartoonist,
at the University of Michigan (1994)

Remember this simple charge—love your soldiers with all your heart and soul and mind and body. And selflessly serve your grateful nation.

—**Colin Powell,** chairman of the Joint Chiefs of Staff, at the United States Military Academy (1990)

Music is probably the oldest religious rite. **Our ancestors used melody and rhythm to co-opt the spirit world to their purposes**—*to try and make sense of the universe. The first priests were probably musicians, the first prayers probably songs.*

—**Sting,** *musician, at the Berklee College of Music (1994)*

So, I went here. Class of '73. Graduated cum laude. In general studies. Harvard was in many ways a different place in those days. It was much whiter, much more male, and much more preppy.

—*Al Franken,* comedian and author,
at Harvard University (2002)

... I have never forgotten that at a moment when red-alert signals were flashing all over the world, and all sorts of people and institutions were running scared, Bard College did the opposite— that it moved towards me, in intellectual solidarity and human concern, and made, not lofty speeches, but a concrete offer of help. I hope you will all feel proud that Bard, quietly, without fanfares, made such a principled gesture at such a time.

—**Salman Rushdie,** author,
at Bard College (1996)

Today, all of you stand on the shoulders of those Harvard graduates and faculty who have come before you and pioneered many of the advances that we take for granted today. You stand on the shoulders of all the Nobel Leaureates from Harvard who have unlocked the secrets behind some of the world's greatest medical mysteries.

—**Hillary Rodham Clinton,** politician,
at Harvard Medical School (1998)

You have been fortunate to study at a college where reason and faith exist together and reinforce one another. **But you're headed into a world where optimists are too often told to keep their ideals to themselves.** *It is your responsibility as educated people to remain optimistic no matter what . . .*

—**Condoleezza Rice,** *secretary of state,*
at Boston College (2006)

Choate has wounded each of you—fatally and decisively. **You have been wounded into a kind of self-awareness**—an awareness of what your responsibilities are to yourself and to other people—a wound that is never going to heal. If you don't pay proper attention to that wound, you're going to be very, very unhappy people.

—**Edward Albee,** playwright,
at Choate Rosemary Hall (1999)

Commencement Fact

The first "yearbooks" were put together in the 17th century as students pasted newspaper clippings, notes, and other such memorabilia into a book. In 1806, Yale University produced the first college yearbook as a means of profiling its graduating class. Thirty-nine years later, the first high school yearbook was created. It was called "The Evergreen" and was created for students in Waterville, New York. In the late 1800s, improvements in printing made yearbooks more affordable and more popular. In the 1980s, video yearbooks were the new trend and a student would be chosen to narrate.

Gaining knowledge is our only hope for survival. Passing that knowledge on to future generations is our most important challenge.

—*George Lucas,* director,
at the University of Southern California (1994)

Appreciating Family and Friends

All parents **believe their children** can do the impossible. They thought it the minute we were born, and *no matter how hard* we have tried to prove them wrong, they all think it **about us now.**

> —*Cathy Guisewite,* cartoonist,
> *at the University of Michigan (1994)*

The first rule in life is: **Cherish your friends and family as if your life depended on it.** *Because it does.*

—**Ann Richards,** *politician,
at Mount Holyoke College (1995)*

And all of us have to remember the brave people who went before and upon whose backs we climbed. **All of us have to remember where we came from** and what it was like then if we are to understand where we are heading and how to get there.

—**Colin Powell,** chairman of the Joint Chiefs of Staff,
at Fisk University (1992)

But you young men have to be instructed, to your passions. So when this is over today—I know your fathers are here, most of them. I want you to run over and grab your father, and lift him up, and kiss him on both cheeks, and say, **"Dad, thank you for my life. Thank you for being here. I love you."** And then you're going to have one of the greatest moments of this graduation.

—**Ray Bradbury,** author,
at the California Institute of Technology (2000)

Every so often you may hear hints from your parents of things they might have done if they hadn't had you. Such as have a lifestyle, for example, or write poetry, or write fiction, or work on their backhand, or travel, and be more interesting people. But we don't mean it. You were the best thing—one of the best things—that came along and happened to us.

—**Garrison Keillor,** broadcaster and writer,
at Gettysburg College (1987)

I suggest, however, that there are **several heroes and heroines here today who should be recognized** and with whom you graduates would like to share your glory … **I congratulate your parents,** and I commend you graduates for your **good judgment in selecting them.**

—**Sandra Day O'Connor,** justice of the Supreme Court,
at Stanford University (2004)

Please forgive them [parents] for their mistakes and imperfections and fully love them and honor them while you can, because the simple truth is that you won't always have them with you as you move further along your life journey.

—**John Mackey,** corporate executive,
at Bentley College (2008)

To sharpen the irony, the qualities in your parents that annoy you today are likely to be exactly the ones that, later on, your kids will point out in you. So, until then, try giving your parents a break and have a sense of humor about all their qualities.

—***John Walsh,*** *art curator,*
at Wheaton College (2000)

For me, this goes all the way back to my grandmother and then right on down the line. She didn't tell my dad, "Now, you go to the study table." No, no. She said, "I'll meet you at the study table." And that's where your good parents and good teachers are.

—**Woody Hayes,** football coach,
at Ohio State University (1986)

I would like to make it clear, in parenthesis, that **I do not blame my parents** for their point of view. There is an expiry date on blaming your parents for steering you in the wrong direction; the moment you are old enough to take the wheel, **responsibility lies with you.**

—**JK Rowling,** author,
at Harvard University (2008)

I charge you not to break the chain that goes back to the primates that evolved what we now separate into bands and music and poetry and speech as a means of extending memory in an individual lifetime and beyond it. I charge you in whatever way you choose to honor the past and to convey its treasures to the young.

—**Robert Pinsky,** poet,
at Stanford University (1999)

No one will ever love you quite like your parents do, and although they have no doubt made plenty of mistakes in helping you to grow up, they've also done the very best job that they knew how to do. They've also made far more sacrifices on your behalf than you will ever really know.

—**John Mackey,** corporate executive,
at Bentley College (2008)

LISTEN WITH AN OPEN HEART AND AN OPEN MIND TO THOSE WHO LOVE YOU THE MOST.

You may hear a grain of truth that will later become the foundation of your entire belief system.

—**Callie Khouri,** writer,
at Sweet Briar College (1994)

Think hard about who you marry. **It's the most important decision you will ever make.**

—**David Brooks,** writer,
at Wake Forest University (2007)

Being alive is absolutely extraordinary and there are endless things to be thankful and grateful for. I try to take a few minutes early in the morning to be very quiet and to appreciate the people I love and to express gratitude in my heart for the many wonderful things that fill my life with joy.

—**John Mackey,** corporate executive, at Bentley College (2008)

You're young and you're bulletproof and invincible. But never underestimate the power of other people's love and prayer.

—**Tony Snow,** journalist, at Catholic University (2007)

You will teach them [your children] by example not to be terrorized by the narrow and parsimonious expectations of the world, a world that often likes to color within the lines when a spray of paint, a scrawl of crayon, is what is truly wanted.

—**Anna Quindlen,** writer, at Mount Holyoke (1999)

At the end of your life, you will never regret not having passed one more test, not winning one more verdict or not closing one more deal. You will regret time not spent with a husband, a child, a friend or a parent.

—**Barbara Bush,** First Lady,
at Wellesley College (1990)

The family is the cornerstone of our society.
More than any other force it shapes the attitude, the hopes, the ambitions, and the values of the child. And when the family collapses it is the children that are usually damaged. When it happens on a massive scale the community itself is crippled.

—**Lyndon B. Johnson,** U.S. president,
at Howard University (1965)

Every year you are out of school you will have more names in your phone book and fewer actual friends.

—*Cathy Guisewite, cartoonist,*
at the University of Michigan (1994)

I don't remember a single date, or quotation or abstruse reference, but I do remember this: I remember singing at the top of my lungs with my arms around a bunch of friends, wobbling down that street right over there, High Street, laughing and singing and vowing the loyalty of the truly inspired and intoxicated. I still pledge allegiance to that particular flag, although I can't remember anything of that night.

—**Jodie Foster,** actress,
at Yale University (1993)

It *always feels* as if friends we made in high school and college *know us better* than friends we made later.

Why is that?

It's because we came to college raw.

—*Marvin Bell,* poet,
at Alfred University (2002)

I have one last hope for you, which is something that I already had at 21. The friends with whom I sat on graduation day have been my friends for life. They are my children's godparents, the people to whom I've been able to turn in times of trouble, friends who have been kind enough not to sue me when I've used their names for Death Eaters.

—**JK Rowling,** author, at Harvard University (2008)

NOTE: Death Eaters are the evil witches and wizards from the Harry Potter series.

Be kind to your friends,
be kind to your family,
be kind to yourselves.

—**Katie Couric,** broadcaster, at Williams College (2007)

You must read to your children, hug your children, and you must love your children. **Your success as a family...** our success as a society depends not on what happens in the White House, **but on what happens inside your house.**

—**Barbara Bush,** First Lady, at Wellesley College (1990)

It's been said that while the United States is beyond doubt a great nation, it remains to be seen if we are a great people, or whether we are perhaps still engaged in the undertaking of becoming a great people. I propose to you that a people is defined and unified not by blood, but by shared memory— a people is held together and identified by what successfully gets passed on from the old ones to be remembered by the young. A people is its memory, its ancestral treasures.

—**Robert Pinsky,** poet,
at Stanford University (1999)

My three years of service connected me to the rest of the world, the world outside myself, and the connection has been permanent. The experience also left me with a firm conviction that beyond the benefits to individuals, connecting and connections are essential for our democratic society to work. And speaking now as a journalist whose job it's been to pay attention to such things, **I have never seen us more disconnected from each other than we are right now.**

—**Jim Lehrer,** journalist and author describing his time
in the Marine Corps, at Harvard University (2006)

You have a special obligation to do something important with the chance they never had. If you do, their sacrifices for you will have all been worthwhile, and I know you will.

—**Ross Perot,** businessman and third-party candidate for president, at Boston University (1994)

At our graduation *we were bound by enormous affection, by our shared experience of a time that could never come again, and, of course, by the knowledge that we held certain photographic evidence that would be exceptionally valuable if any of us ran for Prime Minister.*

—JK Rowling, author, at Harvard University (2008)

Devote yourself to your kids. Nothing else is guaranteed to make you happy.

—**David Brooks,** writer,
at Wake Forest University (2007)

Who Are You and Who Do You Want to Be?

In reality, your happiness has a
lot more to do with *how you see the world*
than how the world sees you.

—*Callie Khouri, writer,*
at Sweet Briar College (1994)

Whatever path you take, whatever field or fields you choose to enter, the one constant you will find is that **moral challenges await you.** At every step you will have to decide who you are. And who you are **will change.**

—**Lee Blessing,** playwright,
at Reed College (2001)

Find out who you are, what you think.
Listen to the sounds of your own heart.

—*Goldie Hawn, actress,*
at American University (2002)

Imitations are redundant.
Yourself is what is wanted.

—**Anna Quindlen,** writer,
at Mount Holyoke (1999)

Your parents may have wanted you, but they did not dream you up. You did that. I'm just urging you to continue the dream you started, because dreaming is not irresponsible. It's first order, human business. It's not entertainment, you know. It's work.

—**Toni Morrison,** author,
at Sarah Lawrence College (1988)

*My mother instilled in her children the values of **independence, individualism, and perseverance.** She stressed the need to perform as best you can and served as my role model and inspiration. **All of us need role models and inspiration in striving towards our goals.** It is critical that you identify the right role models and are **inspired by their words and deeds.***

—**Florence Griffith Joyner,** *Olympic track star, at American University (1994)*

Out of respect for things that I was never destined to do, I have learned that my strengths are a result of my weaknesses, my success is due to my failures, and my style is directly related to my limitations.

—**Billy Joel,** musician, at Fairfield University (1991)

If your dream is a big one you will need help, you will need to be part of a team. Initially, you will follow, but then you will lead. You will never make a good leader unless you have learned to follow.

—**Robert D. Ballard,** oceanographer and founder of the JASON project, at the Worcester Polytechnic Institute (1992)

Indulge the fool in you. Encourage the clown and the laughter that is inside of you.

*—**Ann Richards,** politician, at Mount Holyoke College (1995)*

I hope you live without the need to dominate, and without the need to be dominated. **I hope you are never victims,** but I hope you have no power over other people.

—**Ursula K. Le Guin,** writer, at Mills College (1983)

Honor is not an impossible ideal, something beyond your grasp. Honor is day to day. It's minute by minute. If you have it, you live without question.

—**Dennis Lehane,** writer, at the University of Massachusetts Boston (2004)

Find work that adds to the world instead of depleting it.

—**Wally Lamb,** *writer,*
at Connecticut College (2003)

Leave it to others to have doubts about you.

—**Callie Khouri,** writer,
at Sweet Briar College (1994)

All lives are a struggle against selfishness.

—**John McCain,** politician,
at The New School (2006)

We may as well dream of the world as it ought to be.

—*Toni Morrison, author,*
at Sarah Lawrence College (1998)

Remember, the most important thing about a life is that it is yours and nobody else's. **You cannot live a life for the sake of your family, your parents, your brothers, your sisters, your children.** A life without duty to these loved ones would not be a good life, but a life lived entirely to meet their expectations is not a good life.

—**Michael Ignatieff,** writer,
at Whitman College (2004)

Be courageous in the expression of your beliefs, whatever they might be.

—**Robert Redford,** actor and director,
at Bard College (2004)

You have a choice. You can either be a passive victim of circumstance or you can be the active hero of your own life.

—**Bradley Whitford,** *actor,*
at the University of Wisconsin (2006)

THINK for yrself, LISTEN to yr heart, TUNE IN to yr gut.

—**Suzan-Lori Parks,** writer,
at Mount Holyoke College (2001)

In the years going forward, it will be your reputation—**for integrity, judgment, and other qualities of character**—that will determine your success in life and in business.

—**Alan Greenspan,** Federal Reserve chairman,
at Wharton School (2005)

Create the highest, grandest vision possible for your life because you become what you believe.

—**Oprah Winfrey,** talk show host,
at Wellesley College (1997)

Cynicism masquerades as wisdom, but it is the farthest thing from it. Because cynics don't learn anything. Because cynicism is a self-imposed blindness, a rejection of the world because we are afraid it will hurt us or disappoint us.

—**Stephen Colbert,** comedian and TV personality,
at Knox College (2006)

*So I have just one wish for you—**the good luck to be somewhere where you are free to maintain the kind of integrity I have described,** and where you do not feel forced by a need to maintain your position in the organization, or financial support, or so on, to lose your integrity. **May you have that freedom.***

—*Richard Feynman, physicist,*
at the California Institute of Technology (1974)

And in that opportunity to witness our plight as human beings in the presence of our fear, our mortality, we can choose to hate ourselves, or to love ourselves. We can choose to feel compassion for ourselves. And when we choose compassion for ourselves, we can find compassion for others.

—**Paul Michael Glaser,** actor, director, and AIDS activist, at the Stanford University School of Medicine (2004)

A generation from now, as you watch your children graduate, you will want to be able to say that whatever success you achieved was the result of honest and productive work, and that you dealt with people the way you would want them to deal with you.

—**Alan Greenspan,** Federal Reserve chairman, at Wharton School (2005)

Your calling isn't something that somebody can tell you about. It's what you feel. It's a part of your life force. It is the thing that gives you juice. The thing that you are supposed to do. And nobody can tell you what that is. You know it inside yourself.

—***Oprah Winfrey,*** talk show host, at Howard University (2007)

Whatever you choose, however many roads you travel, I hope that you choose not to be a lady. I hope you will find some way to break the rules and make a little trouble out there. And I also hope that you will choose to make some of that trouble on behalf of women.

—**Nora Ephron,** screenwriter,
at Wellesley College (1996)

Remember, you **cannot be both young and wise.** Young people who pretend to be wise to the ways of the world are **mostly just cynics.**

—**Stephen Colbert,** comedian and TV personality,
at Knox College (2006)

The way to be happy is to like yourself and the way to like yourself is to do only things that make you proud.

—**Marc S. Lewis,** professor of psychology,
at the University of Texas at Austin (2000)

To live is to choose. But to choose well, you must know who you are, what you stand for, where you want to go and why you want to get there.

—**Kofi Annan,** secretary-general of the United Nations,
at the Massachusetts Institute of Technology (1997)

Have the courage to accept that you're not perfect, nothing is, and no one is—and that's OK.

—**Katie Couric,** broadcaster,
at Williams College (2007)

However, for me the insight that has personally helped me the most when dealing with fear has been to understand that *fear is primarily a creation of the mind.* I create it in my mind—it doesn't really exist outside the mind. I can dissolve it there as well.

—**John Mackey,** corporate executive,
at Bentley College (2008)

I'm very grateful that I never wasted any time trying to become somebody else's image of what I should be.

—*Jerry Zucker, director and producer,
at the University of Wisconsin (2003)*

Do what I did—learn to make it on your personality. **Personality** *is the one quality that doesn't fade with time.*

—**Callie Khouri,** *writer,*
at Sweet Briar College (1994)

Nobody else is paying as much attention to your failures as you are. **You're the only ones who are obsessed with the importance of your own life.** To everyone else, it's just a blip on the radar screen, so just move on.

—**Jerry Zucker,** director and producer, relaying the advice
John Travolta gave him after his movie *Top Secret*
received bad reviews, at the University of Wisconsin (2003)

The person who you're with most in life is yourself and **if you don't like yourself** you're always with somebody you don't like.

—**Marc S. Lewis,** professor of psychology,
at the University of Texas at Austin (2000)

It doesn't matter that your dream came true if you spent your **whole life sleeping.**

—**Jerry Zucker,** movie director and producer,
at the University of Wisconsin (2003)

Whether you are 24 or 54, begin today to **say no to the Greek chorus that thinks it knows the parameters of a happy life** when all it really knows is the homogenization of human existence. We need to **eschew that way of being today** more than ever before, to the extent that we have defined ourselves sometimes in this nation in **terms of false gods.**

—**Anna Quindlen,** writer,
at Colgate University (2003)

You are capable of more than you think.
If you've ever smashed a mosquito on your arm, there is a murderous Richard III inside you. If you've ever caught your breath at the sight of someone dipping their toes into Lake Mendota in the late afternoon sun over at the Union, you, too, have Romeo's fluttering heart.

—**Bradley Whitford,** actor,
at the University of Wisconsin (2006)

I hope instead that when you are
"old and gray and full of sleep,"
as the poet William Butler Yeats once
wrote, that you can say that your goal
in life was not the perfection of work alone
but the perfection of a life.

—**Doris Kearns Goodwin,** *presidential historian,*
at Dartmouth College (1998)

Your journey is not over once your goal is reached, your dream fulfilled, the truth attained. The journey is never over until you share what you have learned with others.

—**Robert D. Ballard,** oceanographer

We've been confronted with old problems, and we've met them with old solutions. And I'm hoping somewhere out there is somebody with brand-new ideas.

—**Sherman Alexie,** writer, at the University of Seattle, Washington (2003)

And even today, there are *so many Harvard alumni* here in the United States and around the world who are working to **unlock the secrets** of cancer and research into sickle cell disease, working to rid the world of AIDS and doing so much else. Now it is *your turn to join them.* It is your

time to lead.

—**Hillary Rodham Clinton,** politician, at Harvard Medical School (1998)

We all go through life bristling
at our external limitations,
but the most difficult chains
to break are inside us.

—*Bradley Whitford, actor,*
at the University of Wisconsin (2006)

Learning how to think really means learning how to exercise some control over how and what you think. It means being conscious and aware enough to choose what you pay attention to and to choose how you construct meaning from experience. **Because if you cannot exercise this kind of choice in adult life, you will be totally hosed.**

—*David Foster Wallace,* novelist,
at Kenyon University (2005)

According to a survey of 75 business leaders with Stanford MBAs, the most important predictor of success is **self-awareness.** That means knowing—and accepting—your own strengths and weaknesses.

—**Katie Couric,** broadcaster,
at Williams College (2007)

Moral contamination almost never announces itself; it is always a very small, seemingly silent, inconsequential event, but it is like radiation; it accumulates, and there are no permissible safe levels.

—**E. L. Doctorow,** author,
at Hobart and William Smith Colleges (1979)

Commencement Fact

The purchase of a class ring became a popular practice in the early 20th century, but the first ring was developed a century before for the cadets at West Point. Rings have always been seen as powerful accoutrements. Ancient Egyptians felt that their rings provided eternal life and Roman soldiers believed that their rings would lead them to victory. Traditionally, the class ring was worn on the ring finger of the right hand, but that isn't common practice any more.

"The Real World"

I cannot criticise my parents
for hoping that I would never experience poverty.
They had been poor themselves, and I have since
been poor, and I *quite agree with them*
that it is not an ennobling experience.

Poverty entails fear, and stress,
and sometimes depression; it means
a thousand petty humiliations
and hardships.

—*JK Rowling, author,*
at Harvard University (2008)

Now don't worry about being poor in your twenties. It's a pain, but you can work with it. But later on, it's more difficult, and there's not a lot of glory in being an adult dependent. But, there is a lot of satisfaction in knowing you can make your own way in the world.

—**Callie Khouri,** writer,
at Sweet Briar College (1994)

More than 70 percent of this class had to take out loans to complete the degrees that they receive today. *They will be paying back those loans for a number of years, and I hope that we as a nation will continue to look for ways to provide financial support to students such as these so that they do not have to go into the debt that these young graduates have.*

—***Hillary Rodham Clinton,*** *politician,*
at Harvard Medical School (1998)

When **eating breakfast at a restaurant** and being served by a waitress or a waiter, please know that for breakfast **it is mathematically impossible to over-tip.**

—**Mark Shields,** political analyst,
at Hobart and William Smith Colleges (2002)

Climbing OUt of poverty by your own efforts, that is indeed something on which to pride yourself, but *poverty itself* is **romanticized only by fools.**

—**JK Rowling,** author,
at Harvard University (2008)

If you win the rat race, you will never have trouble feeding your family.

—*Al Franken, comedian and author,*
at Harvard University (2002)

Material possessions **rust away, wear away, or depreciate.** Character alone will never tarnish.

—**Elizabeth Dole,** politician,
at Dartmouth College (1991)

The closed circle of pure materialism is clear to us now—**aspirations become wants, wants become needs, and self-gratification becomes a bottomless pit.**

—**Mario Cuomo,** *politician,*
at Iona College (1984)

To those of you who awoke today in a cold sweat, struck by the realization that **you have no idea what you want to do with the rest of your life,** welcome to the club. I am almost fifty-eight years old, and I do not know what I want to be when I grow up.

—**Jeff Greenfield,** journalist,
at Bucknell University (2002)

You're about to go from 130 vacation days to seven.

—**Donna Shalala,** secretary of health,
at Washington College (2000)

You have played—now comes work.

—*W. E. B. Du Bois, writer and educator,*
at Fisk University (1898)

The tyranny of performing is that the drive is unrelenting and inflexible. It's never good enough; our critics don't even begin to know how inept and awful we feel we are, how undeserving of success, the torture of a constant striving for perfection for actors, historians, composers, writers, choreographers, musicologists, and more—all of you called to the arts, to creativity, and to self-expression.

—**Renée Fleming,** musician,
at The Julliard School (2003)

When people show you who they are, believe them, the first time. Live your life from truth and you will survive everything . . .

—**Oprah Winfrey,** talk show host,
at Wellesley College (1997)

You want to ask yourself, in addition to making a living, raising a family, being part of a community. What is your civic task, where are you going to plant your flag of justice?

—***Ralph Nader,*** *public advocate,*
at Bucknell University (2004)

And in a world where the systems are crushing us, where many of our leaders are shadow-puppets, mouthing hypocrisies on the media stage, where centralization, big business, big government, is constantly, fascistically, gaining each day on the individual and has wiped out so much of the human spirit in this century, **I think that people are the one recurrent hope we have.**

—**Oliver Stone,** director,
at the University of California at Berkeley (1994)

Just like human beings grow up and mature as they understand the realities of life, nations grow up and mature when they understand the realities they actually face.

—**Rudolph Giuliani,** politician,
at Syracuse University (2002)

It was a *myth that's often perpetuated at commencement* that holds that *only hope and promise lie beyond the halls of academe.* Don't worry, be happy. *Everything is fine.*

—*Paul Tsongas, politician,*
at the Massachusetts Institute of Technology (1989)

There's a false assumption out there that talent will surely be recognized. **Just get good at something and the world will beat a path to your door.** Don't believe it. The world is not checking in with us to see what skills we've picked up, what idea we've concocted, **what dreams we carry in our hearts.**

—*Chris Matthews,* broadcaster,
at Fordham University (2006)

Let's get concrete. The plain fact is that you graduating seniors do not yet have any clue what "day in day out" really means. There happen to be whole, large parts of adult American life that nobody talks about in commencement speeches. One such part involves boredom, routine, and petty frustration. The parents and older folks here will know all too well what I'm talking about.

—**David Foster Wallace,** novelist,
at Kenyon College (2005)

You live a life that the one-size-fits-all generations before you can scarcely imagine. **I suspect that you're going to need this spirit of individual inquiry** and self-confidence as you grow along with this country.

—**Anna Quindlen,** writer,
at Colgate University (2003)

If you've got the skills, you've got the education, and you have the opportunity to upgrade and improve both, you'll be able to compete and win anywhere. If not, the fall will be further and harder than it ever was before.

—**Barack Obama,** U.S. president,
at Knox College (2005)

Life is too challenging for external rewards to sustain us. The joy is in the journey.

—**Bradley Whitford,** actor,
at the University of Wisconsin (2006)

But if you really learn how to pay attention, then you will know there are other options. **It will actually be within your power to experience** *a crowded, hot, slow, consumer-hell type situation as not only meaningful, but sacred, on* **fire with the same force that made the stars:** *love, fellowship, the mystical oneness of all things deep down.*

—**David Foster Wallace,** *novelist,*
at Kenyon College (2005)

You are being bequeathed the tools for creating a material existence that neither my generation nor any that preceded it could have even remotely imagined as we began our life's work. **What you must fashion for yourselves are those values that will enable you to contribute and thrive in a world** that is becoming increasingly competitive and frenetic.

—**Alan Greenspan,** Federal Reserve chairman, at Wharton School (2005)

To the centenarian, credit-card living is out, leveraged saving is in. Use your tax leverage to make your savings grow exponentially. In this savings race, the tortoise beats the hare; by taking full advantage of the plans out there now, and more sure to come in the next decade, you need not be a rocket scientist to become a millionaire.

—**David Mahoney,** corporate executive, at Rutgers University (1996)

Know and identify the predators

waving flags made of dollar bills. They will say anything, promise anything, do everything to turn the planet into a casino where only the house cards can win.

—**Toni Morrison,** author, at Wellesley College (2004)

In the business world, everyone is paid in two coins: **cash and experience.** Take the experience first; the cash will come later.

—**Harold Geneen,** founder of
Microwave Communications Inc.

Material success is possible in this world, and far more satisfying, when it comes without exploiting others. **The true measure of a career is to be able to be content, even proud, that you succeeded** through your own endeavors without leaving a trail of casualties in your wake.

—**Alan Greenspan,** Federal Reserve chairman,
at Wharton School (2005)

*If you think education is expensive,
try ignorance!*

—*Andy McIntyre,* producer

Oh this world. Ladies and gentlemen, this world rocks and it never lets up.

—**Patton Oswalt,** comedian,
at his alma mater, Broad Run High School (2008)

Harvard psychologist Daniel Gilbert has spent decades studying happiness and he found that **cash and contentment are almost completely disconnected.** Sure, having money gives you one less thing to worry about, but don't look to it as a magic bullet.

—**Katie Couric,** broadcaster,
at Williams College (2007)

Humanity and Contributing to the Global Good

There is
no community service requirement
in the real world;
no one is forcing you to care.

—*Barack Obama, U.S. president,
at Knox College (2005)*

I want you to consider making your life one **long gift to others...** All that lasts is what you pass on. The rest is smoke and mirrors.

—**Stephen King,** author,
at Vassar College (2001)

You cannot help but learn more as you take the world into your hands. ***Take it up reverently, for it is an old piece of clay,*** *with millions of thumbprints on it.*

—***John Updike,*** *author,*
at the University of Massachusetts, Amherst (1993)

Not everyone can be a philosopher. But every thinking person should reflect on the future and meditate about the destiny of mankind here on earth.

—**Mikhail Gorbachev,** Soviet premier,
at Emory University (1992)

Sometimes I harbor a secret desire to be kidnapped by aliens and taken to a planet more sensible than this one. But time and again hope is renewed by the actions of ordinary people.

—**Christopher Reeve,** actor,
at Middlebury College (2004)

Giving is not something that may interest you right now, **but always remember life is never fulfilled,** *your journey never over until you take time to* **give back a portion** *of what has been given to you.*

—**Robert D. Ballard,** *oceanographer and founder of the JASON project, at the Worcester Polytechnic Institute (1992)*

Except for Native Americans,

we are all immigrants here, and we must learn to **live with one another, among one another, for one another.**

—**Arthur Ashe,** tennis player,
at Kean College (1990)

I have great faith in the strength of intelligence and reason even though I may have a limited amount of either. We have to believe that honest and educated inspection of all our problems is the best way to live successfully. There are a lot of people who don't believe that. They prefer not to face the truth about anything.

—**Andy Rooney,** broadcaster and writer, at Colgate University (1996)

You are your own stories and therefore free to imagine and experience what it means to be human without wealth. What it feels like to be human without domination over others, without reckless arrogance, without fear of others unlike you, without rotating, rehearsing, and reinventing the hatreds you learned in the sandbox.

—**Toni Morrison,** author, at Wellesley College (2004)

Now, I do have faith in the power of humanity to reinvent itself. In this, every graduation offers that possibility.

—**Njabulo S. Ndebele,** poet and activist,
at Wesleyan University (2004)

I understand that many of you have used these uncertain times to explore avenues you might not have considered before—**such as teaching or other forms of public service in troubled communities in the United States or in some of the world's developing countries.** With the ink barely dry, you are coming face-to-face with the unexpected—**the turns of events that engage your passions in ways you never could have predicted or thought possible.**

—**Kofi Annan,** secretary-general of the United Nations,
at Duke University (2003)

There is a whole world awaiting the application of your intelligence, your skills, your ambition, your compassion. **In that regard, how fortunate we are.** Your graduation comes not a moment too soon.

—**Vernon Jordan,** lawyer and business executive,
at the American University School of
Public Affairs/Kogod School of Business (2008)

*Civilizations are judged on their **wars** and their **arts**; that's the measure that's taken.*

*—**Renée Fleming,** musician,
at The Julliard School (2003)*

If you choose to use your status and influence to raise your voice on behalf of those who have no voice; **if you choose to identify** not only with the powerful, but with the powerless; **if you retain** the ability to imagine yourself into the lives of those who do not have your advantages, then it will not only be your proud families who celebrate your existence, but **thousands and millions of people whose reality you have helped transform for the better.**

*—**JK Rowling,** author,
at Harvard University (2008)*

If you don't feed the poor, they will have no choice but to eat you, and the manner of their eating will be as varied as it is ferocious. **They'll eat your houses, your neighborhood, your city, sleep in your lobbies, in your lanes, in your gardens, your intersections.** They'll eat your revenue because there will never be enough prisons and wards and hospitals and welfare hotels to accommodate them.

*—**Toni Morrison,** author,
at Sarah Lawrence College (1988)*

You are in the top one percent of people your age in the world in terms of your education, your health and your ability to make a difference because of the country you live in. . .
Billions of people your age are wondering where they are going to get the next meal and they are doubled over with 20 inches of worm in their gut or they can't speak out because they live in dictatorships or oligarchy.

—**Ralph Nader,** public advocate,
at Bucknell University (2004)

There is no certain road map to success, either for individuals or for generations. **Ultimately, it is a matter of judgment, a question of choice.** *In making that choice, let us remember that there is not a page of American history, of which we are proud, that was authored by a chronic complainer or prophet of despair.* **We are doers.**

—*Madeleine K. Albright, secretary of state, at Harvard University (1997)*

The world badly wants your brains and energy: give them freely, but try to stay conscious of what it is you're giving of yourself and why.

—**John Walsh,** art curator, at Wheaton College (2000)

Humanity's greatest advances are not in its discoveries—but in how those discoveries are applied to reduce inequity. Whether through democracy, strong public education, quality health care, or broad economic opportunity—reducing inequity is the highest human achievement.

—**Bill Gates,** entrepreneur, philanthropist and Harvard dropout, at Harvard University (2007)

Where there is no mandatory duty,
there needs to be a moral imperative.

—**Ralph Nader,** *public advocate,*
at Bucknell University (2004)

For the very first time in our history, it is now possible for a child in the most isolated inner-city neighborhood or rural community to have access to the same world of knowledge at the same instant as the child in the most affluent suburb. Imagine the revolutionary democratizing potential this can bring. Imagine the enormous benefits to our economy, our society, if not just a fraction, but all young people can master this set of 21st century skills.

—**Bill Clinton,** U.S. president,
at the Massachusetts Institute of Technology (1998)

And whenever you're tempted to view the poor or the ill or the persecuted as **"those people"**—people in their own world with their own problems— remember always your neighbors in places like the 9th ward; men and women and children who, just like you, **wanted desperately to escape to somewhere better.**

—**Barack Obama,** U.S. president,
at Xavier University (2006) one year after Hurricane Katrina

We can make the birds stop singing; we can still the fish and make the insects fall from the trees like black rain. **And ironically we've been brought here by reason, by rationality.** We cannot afford to live in a culture that doesn't use the power in its hands with the kind of rationality that produced it in the first place.

—**Alan Alda,** actor,
at the California Institute of Technology (2002)

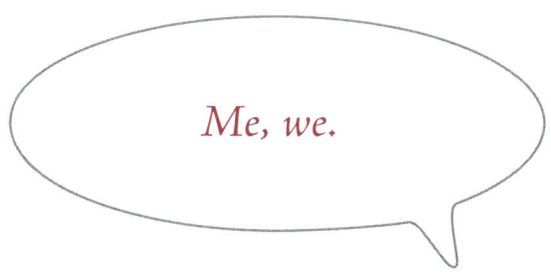

Me, we.

—*Muhammad Ali, boxer,*
at Harvard University (1975)

You are educated. Your certification is in your degree. You may think of it as the ticket to the good life. Let me ask you to think of an alternative. **Think of it as your ticket to change the world.**

—**Tom Brokaw,** broadcaster

Listening isn't passive. It is an act of liberation that will connect you to the world with compassion and be your best guide as you navigate the choppy waters of love, work and citizenship.

—**Bradley Whitford,** actor,
at the University of Wisconsin (2006)

Deep down, we know that what matters in this life is more than winning for ourselves. What really matters is **helping others win** *too.*

—*Fred Rogers, host of the* Mr. Rogers' Neighborhood *television show, at Dartmouth College (2002)*

If you love your families and broaden your reach to care for neighbors and strangers and for our country, then you will send out ripples of hope that will sustain America for your children and their children after them.

—**Federico Peña,** politician,
at the University of Texas (1994)

If we drink from the well,
we have to replenish the well.

—**Steven Spielberg,** director and producer,
at the University of Southern California (1994)

We are all interconnected. As we help others, we cannot help but to help ourselves.

—**Ben Cohen,** *entrepreneur, of Ben & Jerry's, at Southampton College (1995)*

Sympathy is easy. It's always given from a position of power ... **But when you have empathy, you empathize with the person.** You put yourself on equal footing. Sympathy is easy; empathy is hard.

—**Dennis Lehane,** writer, at the University of Massachusetts Boston (2004)

Be creative. *Please give our citizens an alternative to television* **(and especially reality TV)** *as a substitute for anything resembling the creative process.*

—**Renée Fleming,** *musician, at The Julliard School (2003)*

Working for peace and the general welfare is the essence of all true education and all true religion. It is the Sermon on the Mount in action.

—**Henry Wallace,** U.S. vice president, at Connecticut College (1943)

Emerson had something to say about that. He said you can pay back only seldom. But you can always pay forward, and you must pay line for line, deed for deed, and cent for cent. He said beware of too much good accumulating in your palm or it will fast corrupt.

—**Woody Hayes,** football coach, at Ohio State University (1986)

For what is justice? It is to fulfill the fair expectations of man.

—**Lyndon B. Johnson,** *U.S. president, at Howard University (1965)*

I believe passionately that we would all benefit from a full and frank discussion of our mutual responsibilities to serve. Of the joys and satisfactions that come from such service. **From lifting ourselves away from our own needs just for a while** to pay attention to those of others, and of trying to find a way that involves every one of us.

—**Jim Lehrer,** journalist and author, at Harvard University (2006)

Find a mentor and be a mentor. Give back.
And when people tell you not to believe in your
dreams, and they say "Why?", say "Why not?"

—**Billie Jean King,** tennis player,
at the University of Massachusetts Amherst (2000)

Serve,
    serve,
        serve,
for it is the servant that will save us all.

—***Sargent Shriver,*** *philanthropist,*
at Yale University (1964)

Because our individual salvation depends
on our collective salvation.

—**Barack Obama,** U.S. president,
at Xavier University (2006) one year after Hurricane Katrina

**Should the world's most privileged people learn
about the lives of the world's least privileged?**
These are not rhetorical questions—you will answer
with your policies.

—**Bill Gates,** entrepreneur and philanthropist,
at Harvard University (2007)

The really important kind of freedom involves attention and awareness and discipline, and being able truly to care about other people and to sacrifice for them over and over in myriad petty, unsexy ways every day.

—**David Foster Wallace,** *novelist,*
at Kenyon College (2005)

On the plane of international affairs, the outbursts of unreason in this century surpass in horror and human tragedy any the world has seen in the entire modern era ... Our century, even this generation, has much to answer for.

—**Kofi Annan,** secretary-general of the United Nations, at the Massachusetts Institute of Technology (1997)

But the spirit to endure, and to serve, kept him [Schweitzer] going. **And ours is a better world today** because people like Albert Schweitzer, and Mother Teresa, rolled up their sleeves, and **lent a caring hand to those in need.**

—**George H. W. Bush,** U.S. president, at Johns Hopkins University (1997)

The only thing you cannot
be is indifferent.

—*William Styron, author,*
at Augustana College Illinois (2001)

At this time in your life, near the peak of your idealism and possibly as free to experiment, question, pioneer as you may ever be again, many of you may be ready to explore a work where you bring your conscience and time and talent altogether to work every day to improve your society. This is the meaning of citizenship.

—**Ralph Nader,** public advocate,
at Harvard University (1981)

Even though you will fall down and foul up and make mistakes as I have—as everyone does—you will **make this world a better place** if you can bring to it your own unique and individual excellence and quality and originality. This is your gift to give. This is the greatest service you can render to your community and to others.

—**Billy Joel,** musician,
at Fairfield University (1991)

This is America, you. You're America. You're truly its best and its brightest, because you had to work for your education, because you know that just getting this education means someone in the state empathized with you without ever meeting you. And you have to give that empathy back.

—**Dennis Lehane,** writer,
at the University of Massachusetts Boston (2004)

Our country doesn't depend on the heroism of every citizen. But all of us should be worthy of the sacrifices made on our behalf.

—*John McCain, politician,
at The New School (2006)*

Hang your degree on the wall and you have a proud sign of accomplishment, but if you **hang your hat on a cause,** whatever it might be, you will have an investment **that will enrich your life,** your community, your country in both profound and enduring ways.

—**Thomas Ridge,** politician,
at Bucknell University (2005)

The virtue of generosity does not merely apply to giving money, but primarily to the gift of ourselves—our time and our service to others. True generosity should not be thought of as some kind of self-sacrifice where what we give to others comes at our own expense ... Rather it is an extension of love from our own hearts, which takes genuine delight in the flourishing of other people.

—**John Mackey,** corporate executive,
at Bentley College (2008)

With foresight, and a willingness on the part of our people to face up to the vast responsibility which history has clearly placed upon our country, the difficulties I have outlined can and will be overcome.

—**George C. Marshall,** secretary of state and
Army chief of staff, at Harvard University (1947)

We have the talent and the resources and brainpower. But now we need the political will. We need a national commitment.

And we need each of you.

—**Barack Obama,** U.S. president,
at Knox College (2005)

Commencement Fact

In the 1950s, students began to wear gowns that reflected their school colors. However, in higher education, the look of the gown changes depending on the degree that the student has earned. For those receiving a bachelor's degree, the gown has pointed sleeves and a mortar board cap is worn rather than a hood. For those who have earned a master's degree, the gown has long, closed sleeves and a narrow hood. For those who are receiving a doctoral degree, the sleeves of the gown are somewhat bell-shaped and a wide hood is worn. Their hoods are black except for the lining which matches the color(s) of the school and the facing which is determined by the field of study.

This Is Your Time

I need not tell you, gentlemen, that the world situation is very serious. That must be apparent to all intelligent people.

I think one difficulty is that the problem is one of such enormous complexity that the very mass of facts presented to the public by press and radio make it *exceedingly difficult for the man in the street* to reach a clear appraisement of the situation.

—*George C. Marshall, secretary of state and Army chief of staff, at Harvard University (1947)*

For in a real sense, America is essentially a dream, a dream as yet unfulfilled. It is a dream of a land where men of all races, of all nationalities and of all creeds can live together as brothers.

—**Dr. Martin Luther King, Jr.,** civil rights leader, at Lincoln University (1961)

What kind of peace do I mean and what kind of a peace do we seek? **Not a Pax Americana enforced on the world by American weapons of war. Not the peace of the grave or the security of the slave.** *I am talking about genuine peace, the kind of peace that makes life on earth worth living, and the kind that enables men and nations to grow, and to hope, and build a better life for their children . . .*

—*John F. Kennedy, U.S. president, at American University (1963)*

The **Great Society** rests on abundance and liberty for all. It demands an end to poverty and racial injustice, to which we are totally committed in our time.

—Lyndon B. Johnson, U.S. president,
laying the foundation for his Great Society initiative,
at the University of Michigan (1964)

If we are to change this society in the deepest way, then all of us who have been marked for cheap labor, all of us must stand up together. We must resist those efforts that are made to turn us against each other.

*—***Gloria Steinem,** feminist, writer, and publisher, at Smith College (1971)

Let us not use multiculturalism to stereotype any group.

*—***Arthur Ashe,** tennis player, at Kean College (1990)

It is also a time of a vertiginous drop in cultural standards, of virulent anti-intellectualism, and of triumphant mediocrity—**a mediocrity that characterizes the educational system that you have just passed through,** or has passed you through (for all the efforts and good will of many of your teachers). Trivializing standards, using as their justification the ideal of democracy, have made the very idea of a serious humanist education virtually unintelligible to most people.

—**Susan Sontag,** writer and director,
at Wellesley College (1983)

If freedom does not finally reside in the mind, it cannot finally reside anywhere.

—**A. Bartlett Giamatti,** university president and commissioner
of Major League Baseball, at Yale University (1986)

*World peace, like community peace, does not require that each man love his neighbor, it requires only that they **live together in mutual tolerance,** submitting their disputes to a just and peaceful settlement.*

—*John F. Kennedy, U.S. president,
at American University (1963)*

I have come today from the **turmoil** of your capital to the **tranquility** of your campus to speak about the **future** of your country.

—**Lyndon B. Johnson,**
U.S. president, at the
University of Michigan (1964)

We Americans tend to ignore our past. Perhaps we fear having one and burn it behind us like rocket fuel, always looking forward . . .

—**Ken Burns,**
documentary filmmaker,
at Hampshire College (1987)

*Now, if you are a member of a minority group, there is a **limit to the length of time** you can posture yourself as a victim.*

—***Arthur Ashe,*** *tennis player,*
at Kean College (1990)

In your lifetime, this region, which borders five of the world's seven continents, has become the **great meeting place of civilization,** the source of raw materials and the engine of our global economy. Understanding the needs and addressing the concerns of the people of the Pacific rim is becoming not just an important but an essential requirement for our survival and prosperity as a nation.

—**Daniel K. Inouye,** politician, at the University of Hawaii (1992)

*I want to convey the same vision to you today as you graduate into an ethically polluted nation where **instant sex** without responsibility, **instant gratification** without effort, **instant solutions** without sacrifice, getting rather than giving, and **hoarding** rather than sharing are the too-frequent signals of our mass media, popular culture, and political life.*

—**Marian Wright Edelman,** *founder of the Children's Defense Fund, at Washington University (1992)*

The times we live in are indeed alarming. It is a time of the most appalling escalation of violence—violence to the environment, both "nature" and "culture;" violence to all living beings.

—**Susan Sontag,** writer and director,
at Wellesley College (1983)

You graduate as we are taking America's Army and armed forces to the lowest level in fifty years. This will be a post-Cold War force. We will spend less money on defense. **We are going to pay a peace dividend to benefit other parts of our society.**

—**Colin Powell,** chairman of the Joint Chiefs of Staff
and secretary of state, at Fisk University (1992)

At the Carter Center, one of our duties is to monitor—every day—all the conflicts in the world. You might be interested in knowing there are now 112 that we monitor. Thirty-two of these are major wars. A major war by our definition is one within which more than 1,000 people are killed on the battlefield each year. **And in modern-day wars, there are almost ten civilians killed for each soldier killed.**

—**Jimmy Carter,** U.S. president,
at Rice University (1993)

Our technology has developed into formidable, maybe even awesome powers. This technology is **both our opportunity and our danger.** It's a double-edged sword—just as fire was from the beginning . . .

—**Carl Sagan,** astrophysicist,
at Wheaton College (1993)

I am, as I've said, merely competent. But in an age of incompetence, that makes me extraordinary. Maybe that's why I've been able to last in this crazy business. **I actually know how to play my ax and write a song.** That's my job.

—**Billy Joel,** musician,
at the Berklee College of Music (1993)

*Art must challenge the thinking
and fashion of the time and of society.*

—***Oliver Stone,*** *director,*
at the University of California at Berkeley (1994)

To people in the modern world, **true silence is something we rarely experience.** It is almost as if we conspire to avoid it.

—**Sting,** musician,
at the Berklee College of Music (1994)

*The **great lesson of this century** is that what happens to people **anywhere** should matter to people **everywhere**.*

—*Madeleine K. Albright, secretary of state, at Wellesley College (1995)*

We are arguing over the means to better secure our freedom, promote the general welfare and defend our ideals. It should remain an argument among friends; each of us struggling to hear our conscience, and heed its demands; each of us, despite our differences, united in our great cause, and respectful of the goodness in each other. I have not always heeded this injunction myself, and I regret it very much.

—**John McCain,** politician, at The New School (2006)

I would go so far as to say that business is the most powerful force in the world.

This is a new phenomenon which has occurred in my lifetime. Originally the most powerful force in the world was religion. And then the most powerful force came to be government. And today it's business.

—**Ben Cohen,** entrepreneur, of Ben & Jerry's, at Southampton College (1995)

Gene Roddenberry's vision *of the twenty-fourth century was not merely utopianism. It can be part of a blueprint for how we might live, how you might live today.*

*—**Patrick Stewart,** actor,*
at Pomona College (1995)

We desperately need to concentrate on the content of what's being communicated, rather than the method of transportation. **The idea of e-mail is terrific. The thought contained in most messages sent over it is close to zero.**

—**Andy Rooney,** broadcaster and writer,
at Colgate University (1996)

In 1996, like 1896, we really do stand at the dawn of a profoundly new era. I have called it the *Age of Possibility* because of the revolution in information and technology, and market capitalism sweeping the globe, a world no longer divorced by the Cold War.

—**Bill Clinton,** U.S. president,
at Princeton University (1996)

This is your time: the 21st century.
The millennium. It is yours to shape and master. **It makes my heart race. I envy you.**

—**Tom Brokaw,** broadcaster, at Connecticut College (1996)

Don't underestimate how much antagonism there is toward women and how many people wish we could turn the clock back. One of the things people always say to you if you get upset is, don't take it personally, but listen hard to what's going on and, please, *I beg you, take it personally.*

—**Nora Ephron,** screenwriter, at Wellesley College (1996)

Our country, the last remaining superpower on earth, needs to learn to measure its strength **not in how many people we can kill but by how many people we can feed, clothe, house, and care for.** *The enemy is not the poor, and the enemy is not other countries. The enemy is selfishness.*

—*Ben Cohen, entrepreneur, of Ben & Jerry's, at Southampton College (1995)*

We seek a United Nations that will view change as a friend, not change for its own sake but change that permits us to do more good by doing it better. We seek a United Nations that is leaner, more focused, more flexible, and more responsive to changing global needs ...

—**Kofi Annan,** secretary-general of the United Nations, at the Massachusetts Institute of Technology (1997)

Your generation has experienced mass culture with a special intensity.

—***Robert Pinsky,*** *poet, at Stanford University (1999)*

When defending the boldness of the Marshall Plan 50 years ago, Senator Arthur Vandenberg observed that it does little good to extend a **15-foot rope** to a man drowning **20 feet away.** Similarly, we cannot achieve our objectives in Bosnia by doing just enough to avoid immediate war. **We must do all we can to help the people of Bosnia to achieve permanent peace.**

—**Madeleine K. Albright,** secretary of state, at Harvard University (1997)

I asked women to write me their wildest dreams and tell me what their wildest dreams were. Our intention was to fulfill their wildest dreams. We got 77,000 letters, 77,000. To our disappointment we found that **the deeper the wound the smaller the dreams.** So many women had such small visions, such small dreams for their lives that we had a *difficult time coming up with dreams to fulfill.*

—**Oprah Winfrey,** talk show host,
at Wellesley College (1997)

*I know there are many **Star Trek: The Next Generation** fans here. Some who probably know the **Prime Directive** better than me, and though fiction I believe it is an admirable code for any society to listen to. **The Federation of Planets** abolished capital punishment.*

—*Patrick Stewart, actor,
at The Juilliard School (1999)*

You will interact, directly or indirectly, with others just like you across the far reaches of the world. They will represent colleagues, competitors, customers. As you enter this new world, I call upon you to remember this: **as powerful and as progressive a bond that market rationality constitutes, it is not a sufficient basis for human solidarity.**

—**Kofi Annan,** secretary-general of the United Nations, at the Massachusetts Institute of Technology (1997)

As small children *you saw the movie and had the illustrated book, and you pleaded for the spin-off products and you got the action figure and the little figures at the fast-food place, and you saw the cartoon version on television on the weekend.*
By the time you were 14, *manipulated so many times, so effectively, you were more than a little jaded or ironic about mass art, sometimes while being nostalgic about it, at the same time.*

—*Robert Pinsky, poet, at Stanford University (1999)*

As generations go,
mine is not a tough one to follow.

—**Walter Isaacson,** writer,
at Tulane University (2000)

Oh, and it's a media-happy world that wants to rub our noses in the velocity of change. Given the flood of information, and misinformation, and the speed of our society, if you are to stay in touch with your inner self and hold onto your dreams, you will need a sense of proportion, and of ends and means, and of both reality and possibility.

*—**Marvin Bell,** poet,
at Alfred University (2002)*

Then in 2001, the beginning of your junior year, you witnessed our young city's loss of innocence in September just as you began your studies ... Please, remember your legacy of experience. You are extraordinary—*historically unique as a graduating class*—and we need you to be courageous.

—**Renée Fleming,** musician,
at The Julliard School (2003)

I'm not going to talk anymore about the future because I'm hesitant to describe or predict, because **I'm not even certain that it exists.**

—**Toni Morrison,** author,
at Wellesley College (2004)

However, our hindsight does not give us your perspective of this world you're inheriting. Of the greater amount of information you process each day. **Of how it feels to be in your skin,** living cheek to jowl, so much closer through television, computer technology and airplane travel to your fellow man. **Of how it feels to hear so much more acutely the howling vacuum of anonymity.**

—**Paul Michael Glaser,** actor, director, and AIDS activist,
at the Stanford University School of Medicine (2004)

In a **fearful time,** try to be one of the *fearless* ones.

—**Michael Ignatieff,** writer,
at Whitman College (2004)

Conviction

can change the course of history.

—*Jehan Sadat,* widow of Egyptian
prime minister Anwar Sadat,
at Agnes Scott College (2001)

From
the Philosophical
to the Personal

The practical aspect of *nonviolent resistance* is that it exposes the moral defenses of the opponent. Not only that, it somehow **arouses his conscience** at the same time, and it breaks down his morale. He has no answer for it.

—**Dr. Martin Luther King, Jr.,** *civil rights leader, at Lincoln University (1961)*

Personal happiness lies in knowing that **life is not a check-list of acquisition** *or achievement.*

—**JK Rowling,** *author,*
at Harvard University (2008)

"Ready, Fire, Aim."

This is the approach I have used all my life. There are always decisions to be made. In my experience, it is better not to get caught up in over-analysis of a problem.

—**Earl Bakken,** corporate executive,
at the University of Hawaii (2004)

Creativity is allowing yourself to make mistakes. Art is knowing which ones to keep.

—**Jerry Zucker,** director and producer,
at the University of Wisconsin (2003)

Art is not about creating...
It's about being creative in changing the values of our lives.

—*Yoko Ono, artist,*
at the Maine College of Art (2003)

Though I will defend the value of bedtime stories to my last gasp, I have learned to value imagination in a much broader sense. Imagination is not only the uniquely human capacity to envision that which is not, and therefore the fount of all invention and innovation. In its arguably **most transformative** and **revelatory** capacity, it is the power that enables us to empathise with humans whose experiences we have never shared.

—**JK Rowling,** author,
at Harvard University (2008)

I think with movies we can begin to strengthen people's immune systems, because people go into the movies with their defenses down. It's not real, therefore not threatening. When they least expect it, that might be the best time for the guerrillas of art to get in there and move the head and the heart.

—**Oliver Stone,** *director,*
at the University of California at Berkeley (1994)

We believe that societies find their greatness by **encouraging the creative gifts of their people,** not in controlling their lives and feeding their resentments. And we have confidence that people share this vision of dignity and freedom in every culture because liberty is not the invention of Western culture, **liberty is the deepest need and hope of all humanity.**

—**George W. Bush,** U.S. president, at the United States Air Force Academy (2004)

At Whole Foods we practice appreciations at the end of all of our meetings, including even our Board Meetings—**voluntarily expressing gratitude and thanks to our co-workers for the thoughtful and helpful things they do for us.** It would be hard to overestimate how powerful appreciations have been at Whole Foods as a transformational practice for releasing more love throughout the company.

—**John Mackey,** corporate executive, at Bentley College (2008)

*I also remember the twenty-one-year-old Billy Joel and I often wonder what it would be like if we could, somehow, meet each other. **Here I am, forty-two, exactly twice his age.** What would I think of him? . . . **What would he think of me?** Have I fulfilled his dream?*

—**Billy Joel,** *musician,*
at Fairfield University (1991)

Habitat [for Humanity] was a simple idea for volunteers to go out and work side by side with the poorest families in our country. . . There is no charity involved. The family has to put in at least **500 hours on its own house,** one fourth of the total construction time of 2,000 hours. **And they have to pay full price for the house, but they receive interest-free loans.** The Bible says when you lend money to a poor person, *you do not charge interest.*

—**Jimmy Carter,** U.S. president,
at Rice University (1993)

America has always been less secure when freedom is in retreat. America is always more secure when freedom is on the march.

—**George W. Bush,** U.S. president,
at the United States Air Force Academy (2004)

It should not come as a surprise that when I began my involvement in politics, **women made the coffee, and men made the decisions.**

—**Ann Richards,** politician,
at Mount Holyoke College (1995)

When I made coffee and Xeroxed and distributed newspapers at ABC News, I thought my life was over. But I did it; **I didn't complain.** And along the way, I learned a lot, and was ready for the bigger jobs that were around the corner.

—**Katie Couric,** broadcaster,
at Williams College (2007)

We didn't know anything about ice cream so we decided to continue our formal education by taking a correspondence course in ice cream. It was a five-dollar course from Penn State University that we split, so it was **two-fifty apiece.**

—**Jerry Greenfield,** entrepreneur, of Ben & Jerry's,
at Southampton College (1995)

I stand on the stage with the graduates of Connecticut College and the distinguished members of the faculty and the recipients of honorary degrees, and all I can tell you is that **I am living the American dream,** and you have contributed to it.

—**Frank McCourt,** teacher and memoirist, at Connecticut College (1999)

For my mother, playing the piano was the only time that I wasn't the center of her world— **the only time she ignored me.** So I knew something significant—some important ritual— was being enacted here. I suppose I was being initiated into something—initiated into some sort of mystery. The mystery of music.

—**Sting,** musician, at the Berklee College of Music (1994)

When I got married, all my wife's friends said, **"Don't marry him. He's going nowhere."** But I said to her, **"I'm going to the moon, and I'm going to Mars. Do you want to come along?"** And she said, "Yes." She said yes. She took a vow of poverty, and married me.

—**Ray Bradbury,** author, at the California Institute of Technology (2000)

I knew I had to be a journalist

because I'm deeply curious about the world, I love to write, and I saw that when properly practiced, it's a craft that can help galvanize an often complacent citizenry, and *make a difference.*

—**Katie Couric,** broadcaster,
at Williams College (2007)

In my journey of losing a wife and a daughter to AIDS, and then chairing the Elizabeth Glaser Pediatric AIDS Foundation, I found myself talking to and listening to, watching doctors and researchers. I got to see their humanity, often guarded, hidden behind their white coats, and their stethoscopes and microscopes. I got to see how they dealt with what they knew and what they didn't know.

—**Paul Michael Glaser,** *actor, director, and AIDS activist, at the Stanford University School of Medicine (2004)*

The first day I was on the air doing my first talk show back in 1978, it felt like breathing, which is what your true passion should feel like. It should be so natural to you. And so, I took what had been a mistake, what had been perceived as a failure with my career as an anchor woman in the news business and turned it into a talk show career that's done OK for me!

—**Oprah Winfrey,** talk show host,
at Wellesley College (1997)

*Because my parents fled in time, I escaped Hitler. To our shared and constant sorrow, millions did not. **Because of America's generosity, I escaped Stalin. Millions did not.** Because of the vision of Truman-Marshall generation, I have been privileged to live my life in freedom. **Millions have still never had that opportunity.***

*—**Madeleine K. Albright,** secretary of state,
at Harvard University (1997)*

When I was in my 40s, I had no money for an office. I was wandering around UCLA one day... and I heard typing down below—in the basement of the library. And I went down to see what was going on. I found there was a typing room down there. And for **10 cents for a half an hour,** I could rent a typewriter. I said, **"My God. This is great!** I don't have an office. I'll move in here with a bunch of students. And I'll write!" **So, I got a bag full of dimes, and in the next nine days—I spent $9.80—and I wrote *Fahrenheit 451*.**

—**Ray Bradbury,** author,
at the California Institute of Technology (2000)

In the 1950s, I worked as a ticket agent in a Continental Trailways bus depot in a place called Victoria in south Texas. **And one of my duties was to do this into a microphone:** *May I have your attention, please. This is your last call for Continental Trailways 8:10 p.m., Silversides air conditioned Thruliner to Houston now leaving from lane one for Inez, Edna, Ganado, Louise, El Campo, Pierce, Wharton, Hungerford, Kendleton, Beazley, Rosenberg, Richmond, Sugarland, Stafford, Missouri City, and Houston. All aboard."*

—**Jim Lehrer,** journalist and author,
at Harvard University (2006)

And we also learned that when the political environment makes it impossible to take large steps in a direction you believe you must go, then you have either the choice of taking smaller steps or sitting on the sidelines and doing nothing. **I come from the school of smaller steps.** It is far better to try to make changes that will **help at least some people** than to **do nothing and help no one.**

—**Hillary Rodham Clinton,** politician,
at Harvard Medical School (1998)

I felt a tremendous surge of emotion when the news came through. **The Wall's fall was the beginning of the end of the Cold War.** But this wasn't a time to gloat. Hard-liners in the Soviet Union had just suffered an embarrassing set-back, and I didn't want to do or say anything that might provoke a drastic retaliation in Germany—or to jeopardize Gorbachev's shaky position as the force for reform in the USSR. **That's why I also didn't heed the advice of Congressional leaders, some of whom suggested I go to Berlin and dance on the Wall with the students.**

—**George H. W. Bush,** U.S. president,
at Johns Hopkins University (1997)

My grandmother was a maid and she worked for white folks her whole life. And her idea of having a big dream was to have white folks who at least treated her with some dignity, who showed her a little bit respect. *And she used to say, I want you to—I hope you get some good white folks that are kind to you. And I regret that she didn't live past 1963 to see that I did grow up and get some* **really good white folks working for me.**

> —**Oprah Winfrey,** *talk show host,*
> *at Howard University (2007)*

I got married, had children, was a professor at Harvard trying to teach and write and be with my kids, doing nothing right. I finally decided to give up teaching so I could have time to write and be at home with my family. **And even then it still took 10 years to write my second book,** on the Kennedys.

> —**Doris Kearns Goodwin,** presidential historian,
> at Dartmouth College (1998)

But after his [Granddaddy Rice] first year, he didn't have any more money and they told him he was going to have to leave school. And Granddaddy said to a college administrator, **"Well, how are those boys going to school?"** And the administrator said, *"Well, you see, they have what's called a scholarship. And if you wanted to be a Presbyterian minister, then you could have a scholarship, too."* And Granddaddy Rice said, *"You know, that's just what I had in mind,"* and my family has been college educated and Presbyterian ever since.

—**Condoleezza Rice,** secretary of state, at Boston College (2006)

The truth is, **I was afraid the day I walked into Stanford.** *And I was afraid the day I walked out.*

—**Carly Fiorina,** *corporate executive, at Stanford University (2001*

I remember being at a party during this time while still struggling with the book and I overheard somebody say, "Whatever happened to Doris Kearns, anyway?" as if I had died by not being at Harvard anymore and not producing anything. But the book finally came out, and I'd like to think it made no difference to the world how long it took but it mattered to my kids when they were young. It all goes so quickly.

—**Doris Kearns Goodwin,** presidential historian, at Dartmouth College (1998)

Radcliffe was a great place to live. There were more women up there, and most of the guys were science-math types. **That combination offered me the best odds, if you know what I mean.** This is where I learned the sad lesson that improving your odds doesn't guarantee success.

—**Bill Gates,** entrepreneur, philanthropist and Harvard dropout, at Harvard University (2007)

When I boxed, I trained alongside a kid in Upstate New York. The teenager couldn't wait to be champ, and thought ALL would be great when he won the heavyweight title and fulfilled his destiny. This kid COULD NOT MISS. And he actually accomplished what he set out to do. I'm talking about **Mike Tyson.** He found that winning the title was the *beginning* of the journey, not the *end*.

—**Brian Kenny,** sportscaster, at Ohio Northern University (2007)

I was lost and confused, but one day, a wonderful thing happened. ***I wandered into a course on international politics taught by a Czech refugee who specialized in Soviet studies, a man who had a daughter by the name of Madeleine K. Albright.*** *With that one class, I was hooked. I discovered that my passion was Russia and all things Russian. Needless to say, this was* ***not exactly what young black girls from Birmingham were supposed to do*** *in the early 1970s.*

—***Condoleezza Rice,*** *secretary of state, at Boston College (2006)*

My roommate... was going to an orientation meeting at the *Harvard Lampoon,* the school humor magazine, and I decided for some reason to tag along. **I wrote one piece, then I wrote another piece, then another. Before long, I was running the place.** The only difference was, I was *joyously happy.* I was succeeding at something because I loved the process, not because I was trying to get anywhere. **I had found the thing I wanted to do for the rest of my life.**

—**Conan O'Brien,** comedian, writer, and talk show host, at Stuyvesant High School (2006)

I worried that they would realize

I was just a student in a dorm and hang up on me. Instead they said: **"We're not quite ready, come see us in a month," which was a good thing, because we hadn't written the software yet.** From that moment, I worked day and night on this little extra credit project that marked the end of my college education and the beginning of a remarkable journey with Microsoft.

—**Bill Gates,** entrepreneur, philanthropist and Harvard dropout, recalling his first deal, at Harvard University (2007)

On the Lighter Side

Please be assured that I am well aware that the *least relevant* person involved at a commencement is the
commencement speaker.

—*Jim Lehrer, journalist and author, at the University of Pennsylvania (2002)*

My job is to bore you
and let the hardness of your seat and
the warmth of your robe prepare you for
what is to come.

—**William McNeill,** *history professor,*
at Bard College (1984)

This is not the Worcester, Mass Boat Show, is it? I
am sorry. I have made a terrible mistake.
Ever since I left *Saturday Night Live,* I mostly do
public speaking now. *And I must have made an
error in the little Palm Pilot.* Boy. Don't worry.
I got it on me. I got the speech on me …

—**Will Ferrell,** comedian and actor,
at Harvard University (2003)

The fact that the University of Michigan would
have a commencement speaker **who has publicly
admitted to hiding in the ladies' room with
a box of doughnuts** as a way of coping with
business pressure means a lot to me.

—**Cathy Guisewite,** cartoonist,
at the University of Michigan (1994)

"Commencement speakers," said Father Flynn, *"should think of themselves as the body at an old-fashioned Irish wake.* They need you in order to have the party, but nobody expects you to say very much."

—**Mario Cuomo,** *politician, quoting the advice given to him by Father Flynn of St. John's University, at Iona College (1984)*

I am somewhere between feeling important to be speaking to you on such a significant day in your lives and ridiculous to be standing here in this costume. **I, at least, *unlike some of you,* probably, have something on under this besides** my Jockey shorts.

—**Andy Rooney,** broadcaster and writer, at Colgate University (1996)

In fact, outsourcing is so easy that I had this speech today written by a young man named Panjeeb from Bangalore. **If you don't like the jokes, I assure you they were much funnier in Urdu...**

—**Stephen Colbert,** comedian and TV personality, at Knox College (2006)

*Graduation is a time for words of wisdom, thought-provoking words, challenging words. **And that is why we have Ben with us today.** I'll be speaking to you about how we reached our august positions as true ice-cream magnates.*

—**Jerry Greenfield,** *entrepreneur, of Ben & Jerry's, at Southampton College (1995)*

The authorities of Connecticut College have informed me that for me to **speak longer than twenty minutes** would be regarded as **cruel and inhuman punishment** and that if I go as long as thirty minutes, several strong men will mount this platform and forcibly remove me. But if I can finish in **fifteen minutes,** they will let me **stay for lunch.**

—**Russell Baker,** writer, at Connecticut College (1995)

I have thought long and hard about how to advise you, inspire you, thrill and excite you over multiple speakers that repeat each word-erd-erd in that sonic-onic-onic Doppler-oppler-oppler effect-ect-ect that makes you want to go to sleep-eep-eep.

—**Meryl Streep,** actress, at the University of New Hampshire (2003)

I applaud the graduates today for taking a much more direct route to your degrees. For my part, I'm just happy that the *Crimson* has called me **"Harvard's most successful dropout."** I guess that makes me valedictorian of my own special class . . . I did the best of everyone who failed.

—**Bill Gates,** entrepreneur, philanthropist and Harvard dropout, at Harvard University (2007)

In preparation for today, I read a number of other commencement addresses. **There seems to be an obligatory reference to Aldous Huxley's *Brave New World*.** And also to give the perception that you are intelligent, you don't actually have to BE intelligent, but just create the perception. This can usually be accomplished by a reference to Kafka—**even if you have never read any of his. . . or her** works.

—**Bob Newhart,** actor and comedian, at Catholic University (1997)

*Commencement speeches were invented largely in the belief that outgoing college students should never be released into the world until they have been **properly sedated.***

—*G. B. Trudeau, cartoonist, in a Doonesbury comic strip*

Graduation exercises, like this one, embody one of the great secular rituals in our culture, unique and strange occasions involving funny hats which some here have made funnier and more light-hearted and more individual and more festive with pineapples and inflatable surgical gloves and trees and things I don't know what they are.

—**Robert Pinsky,** poet,
at Stanford University (1999)

A graduation ceremony is an event where the commencement speaker tells thousands of students dressed in identical caps and gowns that "individuality" is the key to success.

—**Robert Orben,** comedy writer and magician

Yes, you're a glorious beautiful rainbow of brainiacs. And that can be very intimidating, let's face it, most of you are smarter than me. It's a proven fact that as you get older, your brain shrinks and you get dumber. This is why you have to explain to your parents how a TIVO works and they have to explain to your grandparents how a cat works.

—**Conan O'Brien,** comedian, writer, and talk show host,
at Stuyvesant High School (2006)

Today, Stuyvesant has a remarkably diverse and varied student body, **ranging from math geeks to science nerds.**

—**Conan O'Brien,** comedian, writer, and talk show host,
at Stuyvesant High School (2006)

Graduation day is tough for adults.
They go to the ceremony as parents. They come home as contemporaries. After twenty-two years of childraising, they are now unemployed.

—**Erma Bombeck,** humor columnist

People will frighten you about a graduation... They use words you don't hear often: **"And we wish you Godspeed."** It is a warning, Godspeed. It means you are no longer welcome here at these prices.

—**Bill Cosby,** actor and comedian,
at Southern Methodist University (1995)

I'm a bad influence. That's why I was invited to speak at your graduation. If I had spoken at your orientation, fewer of you might be here today.

—*Bill Gates, entrepreneur, philanthropist and
Harvard dropout, at Harvard University (2007)*

I'm being paid for this, right?

Oh, wait, there's some advice, right off the bat–always get paid. **If you make enough money in this world you can smoke pot all day and have people killed.** I'm sorry, that was irresponsible. You shouldn't have people killed. **Boom! Marijuana endorsement eleven seconds into my speech!** Too late to cancel me now! It's dumb-ass remarks like that which kept me out of the National Honor Society. . .

—**Patton Oswalt,** comedian,
at his alma mater, Broad Run High School (2008)

You women should only have to do **half the housework.** It's only fair that **your mum should do the other half.**

—**Sacha Baron Cohen,** comedian, discussing feminism
in the character of Ali G, at Harvard University (2004)

I have been led to understand that tomorrow you are going to graduate. Well, my strong recommendation is that you don't go. **Stop! Go on back to your rooms. Unpack!** *There's not much out here.*

—**George Plimpton,** *writer,
at Harvard University (1997)*

The closest I ever got to that world was playing the role of a doctor. A Dr. Peter Chernak on the soap opera, *Love of Life*. **He fought the establishment, slept on a cot in his lab, cooked polish sausages over a Bunsen burner, and seduced the nurses. Not bad!** He also had the ability to heal people whenever the writers felt like it.

—**Paul Michael Glaser,** actor, director, and AIDS activist,
at the Stanford University School of Medicine (2004)

The first thing I would like to say is "thank you." *Not only has Harvard given me an extraordinary honour, but the **weeks of fear and nausea I've experienced at the thought of giving this commencement address have made me lose weight.** A win-win situation! Now all I have to do is take deep breaths, squint at the red banners and fool myself into believing I am at the world's **best-educated Harry Potter convention.***

—*JK Rowling, author,*
at Harvard University (2008)

I congratulate all the parents who are here. It's a glorious day when your child graduates from college. **It's a great day for you; it's a great day for your wallet.**

—**George W. Bush,** U.S. president,
at Yale University (2001)

> *What did Lincoln give America, apart from the Town Car?*

—**Sacha Baron Cohen,** comedian,
discussing presidential history in the character
of Ali G, at Harvard University (2004)

I entered Syracuse University with the class of '51, dropped out after two years, and am finally receiving my degree with the class of '78. **There is hope for slow learners.**

—**William Safire,** journalist,
at Syracuse University (1978)

Professors, of course, are always different. That's what makes them so easy to imitate at parties.

—**Marvin Bell,** poet,
at Alfred University (2002)

I judge the academic excellence of a college in inverse ratio to the success of its football team. By those standards Colgate is one of the outstanding academic institutions in America. That's what we get for letting the students play.

—**Andy Rooney,** broadcaster and writer,
at Colgate University (1996)

I graduated from Mount Holyoke in 1985. Here I am 16 years later. The learned faculty is seated there behind me, and so, before I get into the swing of things, I want to state that any grammatical errors, historical fabrications and inappropriate flights of fancy contained within the following speech are the sole responsibility of the Commencement Speaker and, if found objectionable, should in no way be viewed as an example of the caliber of education one would receive at Mount Holyoke College.

—**Suzan-Lori Parks,** writer,
at Mount Holyoke College (2001)

I wish you much joyful weirdness in your lives.

—*Gary Larson, cartoonist,
at Washington State University (1990)*

Now don't hang on, nothing lasts forever but the Harvard **alumni endowment fund.** It adds up, has performed at 22 percent growth over the last six years.

Dust in the wind, you're so much more than dust in the wind.
Dust in the wind, you're shiny little very smart pieces of dust in the wind.

—**Will Ferrell,** comedian and actor, singing at Harvard University (2003)

There are *so many challenges facing this next generation,* and as they said earlier, you are up for these challenges. **And I agree, except that I don't think you are. I don't know if you're tough enough to handle this. You are the most coddled generation in history.** I belong to the last generation that *did not have to be in a car seat.* You had to be in car seats. I *did not have to wear a helmet* when I rode my bike. You do. **You have to wear helmets when you go swimming, right?**

—**Stephen Colbert,** comedian and TV personality, at Knox College (2006)

It is a great pleasure to be with you today at your commencement exercises. After all, it is a day of joy for everyone: You graduates have no more exams or classes to endure. **And I might say, the faculty no longer has you to endure.**

—**Sandra Day O'Connor,** *justice of the Supreme Court, at Stanford University (2004)*

Before I start, how many of you here today read me in high school? How many? **You're all my bastard children, aren't you?** Thank you, thank you for that.

—**Ray Bradbury,** author,
at the California Institute of Technology (2000)

It [Life] will not be anything like what you think it will be like, but surprises are good for you. **And don't be frightened: you can always change your mind.** I know: **I've had four careers and three husbands.**

—**Nora Ephron,** screenwriter,
at Wellesley College (1996)

To those of you who are here from the class of '97, I say congratulations. **You may be in debt, but you made it.** *And if you're not in debt now, after the alumni association gets through with you,* **you will be.**

—**Madeleine K. Albright,** secretary of state, at Harvard University (1997)

You who have worked so hard to pack your heads with learning until **your skulls are all plump like—sausage of knowledge.** It's an apt metaphor, don't question it.

—**Stephen Colbert,** comedian and TV personality, at Knox College (2006)

Thank you Mr. President, I had forgotten how crushingly dull these ceremonies are. Thank you. My best to the choir. I have to say, that song never grows old for me. Whenever I hear that song, it reminds me of nothing.

—**Jon Stewart,** talk show host and comedian, poking fun at a school song at the College of William and Mary (2004)

A few of you have followed in the path of the perfect West Point graduate, Robert E. Lee, who never received a single demerit in four years. Some of you followed in the path of the imperfect graduate, Ulysses S. Grant, who had his fair share of demerits, and said the happiest day of his life was "the day I left West Point." During my college years I guess you could say I was a Grant man.

—**George W. Bush,** U.S. president,
at the United States Military Academy (2002)

Never argue with an idiot.

—**Callie Khouri,** writer,
at Sweet Briar College (1994)

Of course there's a lot of knowledge in universities: the freshmen bring a little in; the seniors don't take much away, so knowledge sort of accumulates.

—*A. Lawrence Lowell, president of Harvard University*

What piece of wisdom can I impart to you about my journey that will somehow ease your **transition from college back to your parents' basement?**

—**Jon Stewart,** talk show host and comedian,
at the College of William and Mary (2004)

In 1969, girls were admitted to Stuyvesant for the first time. This started a new trend among the boys called showering. You didn't want to be here pre-1969.

—**Conan O'Brien,** *comedian, writer, and talk show host,
at Stuyvesant High School (2006)*

Somewhere out in this audience may even be someone who will one day follow in my footsteps, and preside over the White House as the President's spouse. . . I wish him well!

—**Barbara Bush,** First Lady,
at Wellesley College (1990)

To those of you who received honors, awards and distinctions, I say well done. **And to the C students, I say you too may one day be president of the United States.**

—**George W. Bush,** U.S. president,
at Yale University (2001)

I've found that one other thing that humor does is it makes us free. *That may seem like an odd conclusion, but as long as the tyrant cannot control the minds of free men, they remain free. . .*

—**Bob Newhart,** *actor and comedian,*
at Catholic University (1997)

Your families are extremely proud of you. You can't imagine the sense of relief they are experiencing. **This would be a most opportune time to ask for money.**

—**Gary Bolding,** art professor,
at Stetson University (1998)

People will tell you that your future depends on what major you choose. **This is not true. Einstein majored in hotel management. Dick Cheney majored in modern dance,** *and* Britney Spears wrote a thesis on socialist labor relationships in post-glasnost Poland.

—**Conan O'Brien,** comedian, writer, and talk show host, at Stuyvesant High School (2006)

Humor is also our way of dealing with the inexplicable. We had an earthquake a couple of years ago in Los Angeles, and it wasn't more than three or four days later that I heard the first earthquake joke. Someone said, *"The traffic is stopped, but the freeways are moving."*

—**Bob Newhart,** actor and comedian, at Catholic University (1997)

About the Big Day

I always find it a **challenge** to deliver a *commencement address.* The **parents** who are here would like a speech that is **somewhat sentimental.** The **faculty** would like a speech that is **substantive.** And the **graduates** want a speech that is, well, **short.**

—**William Cohen,** *secretary of defense, at the United States Naval Academy (1999)*

Without question, we share the intense desire for the speech to end and the party to begin.

—**Colin Powell,** *chairman of the Joint Chiefs of Staff, at the United States Military Academy (1990)*

To the parents of the Class of '97, I know how you feel. I have had three daughters graduate from college, and always the emotions are mixed. You feel one part sad, one part relieved, one part broke, and every part proud.

—**Madeleine K. Albright,** secretary of state, at Mount Holyoke College (1997)

It did, however, come to my attention that Roger Clemens and Woody Allen were also under consideration to give this address. Well, let me reassure you that **I happen to possess the fastball of Woody Allen and certainly the existential angst of Roger Clemens.**

—**Ken Burns,** documentary filmmaker, at Hampshire College (1987)

Commencement speakers have a good deal in common with **grandfather clocks:** *Standing usually some six feet tall, typically ponderous in construction, more traditional than functional,* **their distinction is largely in their noisy communication of essentially commonplace information.**

—**W. Willard Wirtz,** secretary of labor,
at the University of Iowa (1965)

Nothing is as easy to make *as a promise this* **winter** *to do something next* **summer;** this is how commencement speakers are caught.

—**Sydney J. Harris,** journalist

The commencement speech is not, I think, a wholly satisfactory manifestation of our culture.

—**John Kenneth Galbraith,** economist,
at American University (1984)

I tried to get out of this ceremony seventeen years ago... because I was twenty-two and **I was way too cool to put on a goofy Batman outfit and a paper plate on my head ...** and listen to a bunch of boring geriatrics tell me how it was up to the youth of America to save the world.

—**Barbara Kingsolver,** author,
at the University of Maine (1998)

The best thing you can give yourselves
for graduation is the gift of possibility.

—**Paul Newman,** actor,
at Sarah Lawrence College (1989)

*Take plenty of pictures. It's a great day,
and one you can never repeat.*

—**John Grisham,** *author,*
at Mississippi State University (1992)

Try to make sure that this moment becomes a **tradition** in **your family,** for **your children** and **your children's children.**

—**Michael Ignatieff,** writer,
at Whitman College (2004)

They [commencements] are a time when hopes are set free with so much future before us that hopes can be infinite.

—**Gloria Steinem,** feminist, writer, and publisher, at Wellesley College (1993)

As a former professor and current mother, I confess to loving graduation days—*especially when they are accompanied by an honorary degree.* I love the ceremony; I love the academic settings; and although it will be difficult for me today—let's be honest—I love to daydream during the commencement speech.

—**Madeleine K. Albright,** secretary of state, at Harvard University (1997)

We have come to take part in the handing over of special emblematic objects, diplomas, which bear language dimly understood or downright incomprehensible inscribed on unfamiliar materials signed and stamped with seals so formal they're nearly mystical with symbols and mottoes.

—**Robert Pinsky,** *poet, at Stanford University (1999)*

You've had a wonderful opportunity to become educated people, but what really matters is not what you have learned and not what is said to you on this day, but what you do with all the days ahead of you.

—**Condoleezza Rice,** secretary of state,
at Boston College (2006)

*Graduation is a time of completion, of finishing, of an ending, however, it is also a time of **celebration of achievement** and a beginning for the new graduate.*

—***Catherine Pulsifer,*** *author and blogger*

These are moments to be cherished in America life: **The realization of a common dream, unique, really, to this land—a college education, a privilege not confined to the well-born or wealthy.** Here the working class sits side by side with old and new fortunes; here new Americans from distant lands and cultures mingle with the **sons and daughters of Americans who came on sailing ships, some to proclaim their freedom, others in the holds and chains of slave ships.**

—**Tom Brokaw,** broadcaster,
at Connecticut College (1996)

There is a good reason they call these ceremonies "commencement exercises." Graduation is not the end; it's the beginning.

—**Orrin Hatch,** politician

To the Class of 2002, big congratulations. You made it to the finish line. You also made it to the start line. After the long good-bye, **the big hello.**

—***Marvin Bell,*** *poet,*
at Alfred University (2002)

Don't think this is the end of your education because it's only the beginning. **They don't call it commencement for nothing.**

—**Andy Rooney,** broadcaster and writer,
at The College of Wooster (2001)

Graduation is one of the few genuine rites of passage left in our society. You are, individually and collectively, passing symbolically from one place to another, from an old to a new status. **And, like all such rites, it is both retrospective and prospective.**

—**Susan Sontag,** author, screenwriter, and director,
at Wellesley College (1983)

Colleges and universities are places where those fundamental activities—taking care of the offspring, revering the ancestors—come together in a single effort. Commencement exercises are a sort of transition or meeting place between those two broad purposes. **If you come on a tribe that neglects its children or ignores its old ones, you know that some tremendous woe is about to extinguish that people's spirit.**

> —**Robert Pinsky,** poet,
> at Stanford University (1999)

Despite my special stature as a rare Indian, I didn't go through my graduation ceremony. And I regret that all the time. I didn't participate in this amazing and sacred ceremony. So I want to thank all of you graduates today for allowing me to be a part of your amazing and sacred ceremony.

> —*Sherman Alexie, writer,*
> *at the University of Seattle, Washington (2003)*

Commencement Fact

According to the National Center for Education Statistics, more than three million high school students graduated with the class of 2008. From public schools there were approximately 2,988,000 graduates, while 315,000 students graduated from independent schools.

Quotes *for* Graduation Speeches

The roots of education
are bitter, but the fruit is sweet.

—*Aristotle*

An investment in knowledge
always pays the best interest.

—**Benjamin Franklin**

Education is what survives when what has been learned has been forgotten.

—**B. F. Skinner**

Education is an admirable thing, but it is well to remember from time to time that **nothing worth knowing can be taught.**

—*Oscar Wilde*

The advantage of a *classical education* is that it enables you to **despise the wealth** that it *prevents you from achieving.*

—**Russell Green**

A man who has never gone to school may steal from a freight car; but if he has a university education, he may steal the whole railroad.

—**Theodore Roosevelt**

The important thing is not to stop questioning.

—**Albert Einstein**

The larger the island of knowledge,
the longer the shoreline of wonder.

—*Ralph W. Sockman*

The one real object of education is to
have a man in the condition of continually asking
questions.

—Bishop Mandell Creighton

The whole purpose of education is to
turn mirrors into windows.

—Sydney J. Harris

*To the uneducated, an A is **just three sticks.***

—*A. A. Milne*

It takes most men **five years to recover from a
college education,** and to learn that poetry is as vital
to thinking as knowledge.

—Brooks Atkinson

The things taught in schools and colleges are not
an education, but the **means of education.**

—Ralph Waldo Emerson

A professor is someone who talks in someone else's sleep.

—**W. H. Auden**

I learned law so well, the day I graduated **I sued the college,** won the case, and got my tuition back.

—**Fred Allen**

*Nothing is more important for the public welfare than to form and train our youth in **wisdom and virtue.***

—*Benjamin Franklin*

Real education should educate us out of self into something far finer; into a selflessness which links us with all humanity.

—**Nancy Astor**

The trouble with learning from experience is that you **never graduate.**

—**Doug Larson**

Life is my college. May I graduate well,
*and earn some **honors!***

— *Louisa May Alcott*

Education is the best provision for old age.

—Aristotle

In youth we **learn**; in age we **understand**.

—**Marie von Ebner-Eschenbach**

It takes courage to grow up
and become who you really are.

— *e.e. cummings*

How many cares one loses when one decides
not to be ***something*** but to be ***someone***.

—**Gabrielle "Coco" Chanel**

The true meaning of life *is to plant trees,*
under whose shade you do not expect to sit.

—*Nelson Henderson*

The future belongs to those who believe in the
beauty of their dreams.

—**Eleanor Roosevelt**

Sooner or later we all discover that the important moments in life are not the advertised ones, not the birthdays, the graduations, the weddings, not the great goals achieved. **The real milestones are less prepossessing.** They come to the door of memory unannounced, stray dogs that amble in, sniff around a bit and simply never leave. Our lives are measured by these.

—Susan B. Anthony

My father always told me, *"Find a job you love and you'll never have to work a day in your life."*

—Jim Fox

Life consists not in holding good cards but in playing those you hold well.

—Josh Billings (pseudonym of Henry Wheeler Shaw)

There is just one life for each of us:
our own.

—Euripides

We know what we are, **but know not what we may be.**

—William Shakespeare

You can't do anything about the length of your life, **but you can do something about its width and depth.**

—**H. L. Mencken**

The best helping hand that you will ever receive is the one at the **end of your own arm.**

—**Fred Dehner**

Obstacles are those frightful things you see when you take your eyes off your goal.

—*Henry Ford*

A wise man will make more opportunities than he finds.

—**Francis Bacon**

There are no **shortcuts** to any place worth going.

—**Beverly Sills**

Whenever it is possible, a boy should choose some occupation which he should do even if he did not need the money.

—*William Lyon Phelps*

Keep in mind that neither success nor failure is ever **final**.

—**Roger Babson**

Wise are those who learn that **the bottom line** doesn't always have to be their top priority.

—**William Arthur Ward**

Be who you are and say what you feel, because those who mind don't matter and those who matter don't mind.

—*Dr. Seuss*

*Always be a **first-rate version of yourself**, instead of a **second-rate version of somebody else**.*

—*Judy Garland*

Don't waste time learning the "tricks of the trade." **Instead, learn the trade.**

—Attributed to both
James Charlton and **H. Jackson Brown, Jr.**

A college education is not a quantitative body of
memorized knowledge salted away in a card file.
It is a taste for knowledge, a taste for philosophy,
if you will; a capacity to explore, to question to
perceive relationships, between fields of knowledge
and experience.

—**Whitney Griswold**

Try to learn **something about everything**
and **everything about something.**

—*Thomas Henry Huxley*

If you concentrate on what you don't have,
you will never, ever have enough.

—**Oprah Winfrey**

It's important to watch what you put in **your mind.**

—**Linda Knight**

*If you feel that you have both feet planted
on level ground,* **then the university has
failed you.**

—*Robert Goheen*

Surely the shortest commencement address in history—and for me one of the most memorable—was that of Dr. Harold E. Hyde, President of New Hampshire's Plymouth State College. He reduced his message to the graduating class to these three ideals: "Know yourself" - Socrates. "Control yourself" - Cicero. "Give yourself" - Christ.

—**Walter T. Tatara**

Do not follow where the path may lead.
**Go, instead, where there
is no path and leave a trail.**

—**Ralph Waldo Emerson**

*Don't judge each day by the harvest you reap but by **the seeds that you plant.***

—*Robert Louis Stevenson*

Try not to become a **man of success,** but rather try to become a **man of value.**

—**Albert Einstein**

Wherever you go, no matter what the weather, always bring your own sunshine.

—*Anthony J. D'Angelo*

If you aren't fired with enthusiasm, you will be fired with enthusiasm.

—**Vince Lombardi**

Things turn out best for the people who make the best out of **the way things turn out**.

—**Art Linkletter**

*When you dance, **your purpose is not to get to a certain place on the floor.** It's to enjoy each step along the way.*

—*Wayne Dyer*

When people talk, listen completely. Most people never listen.

—**Ernest Hemingway**

*Health is the greatest gift, **contentment** the greatest wealth, **faithfulness** the best relationship.*

—***Buddha***

There's only one corner of the universe you can be certain of improving, and that's your own self.

—**Aldous Huxley**

Don't go around saying the world owes you a living. The world owes you nothing. It was here first.

—Mark Twain

You must try to generate happiness within yourself. If you aren't happy in one place, chances are you won't be happy anyplace.

—Ernie Banks

You miss 100% of the shots you never take.

—Wayne Gretzky

One of the most responsible things you can do as an adult is to become more of a child.

—Wayne Dyer

Hitch your wagon to a star.

—Ralph Waldo Emerson

If you do not tell the truth about yourself **you cannot tell it about other people.**

—Virginia Woolf

Be yourself. The world worships the original.

—Ingrid Bergman

You must be the change you wish to see in the world.

—**Mohandas Gandhi**

Never spend your money **before you have it.**

—**Thomas Jefferson**

Excellence is not a skill. It is an attitude.

—*Ralph Marston*

Service is the rent that you pay for room on this earth.

—**Shirley Chisholm**

Wherever you go, go with all your heart.

—**Confucius**

What lies behind us and what lies before us are tiny matters compared to what lies within us.

—*Ralph Waldo Emerson*

Shoot for the moon. Even if you miss, you'll land among the stars.

—**Les Brown**

Twenty years from now you will be more disappointed by the things you didn't do than by the ones you did. So throw off the bowlines, sail away from the safe harbor. Catch the trade winds in your sails.

Explore.

Dream.

Discover.

—Mark Twain

Think big thoughts but relish small pleasures.

—H. Jackson Brown, Jr.

To be nobody but yourself in a world which is doing its best, night and day, to make you everybody else means to **fight the hardest battle which any human being can fight; and never stop fighting.**

—e.e. cummings

Make the most of yourself,

for that is all there is of you.

—Ralph Waldo Emerson

It is not the mountain we conquer but ourselves.

—Edmund Hillary

Your playing small does not serve the world. There is nothing enlightened about shrinking so that other people won't feel insecure around you. We are all meant to shine, as children do.

—**Marianne Williamson**

*Success isn't a result of spontaneous combustion. **You must set yourself on fire.***

—Arnold H. Glasow

Don't be afraid to take a big step if one is indicated; **you can't cross a chasm in two small jumps.**

—**David Lloyd George**

You can't live a perfect day
without doing something for someone who will never be able to repay you.

—**John Wooden**

If you can imagine it, you can achieve it; if you can dream it, you can become it.

*—**William Arthur Ward***

Go for it now. The future is promised to no one.

—**Wayne Dyer**

Success is the ability to go from one failure to another **with no loss of enthusiasm.**

—**Winston Churchill**

Have no fear of perfection—
you'll never reach it.

—*Salvador Dali*

It is not just in some of us; it is in everyone. And as we let our own light shine, we unconsciously give other people permission to do the same. **As we are liberated from our own fear, our presence automatically liberates others.**

—**Marianne Williamson**

As long as you're going to be thinking anyway, **think big.**

—**Donald Trump**

Take calculated risks. That is quite different from being rash.

—*George S. Patton*

From kindergarten to graduation, *I went to public schools,* and I know that they are a key to being sure that every child has a chance to succeed and to rise in the world.

—**Dick Cheney**

Education is a companion which no misfortune can depress, no crime can destroy, no enemy can alienate, no despotism can enslave. At home, a friend, abroad, an introduction, in solitude a solace and in society an ornament. It chastens vice, it guides virtue, it gives at once grace and government to genius. Without it, what is man?

—Joseph Addison

INDEX

Welch, Jack, 19
Westheimer, Ruth, 16, 18
Whitford, Bradley, 18, 21, 33,
 94, 100, 102, 112, 126
Wiesel, Elie, 65
Wilde, Oscar, 197
Williamson, Marianne,
 210, 211
Winfrey, Oprah, 44, 50, 53, 68,
 95, 96, 109, 147, 160, 163,
 204

Wirtz, W. Willard, 189
Wolfe, Tom, 61
Wooden, John, 33, 210
Woolf, Virginia, 207

Z

Zucker, Jerry, 16, 45, 57, 98,
 99, 153